THE LIVING WORD COMMENTARY

Editor
Everett Ferguson

The Gospel
According to Luke

Part I
1:1—9:50

The Gospel According to Luke

Part I
1:1—9:50

Anthony Lee Ash

πᾶσα γραφὴ
θεόπνευστος

SWEET PUBLISHING COMPANY

Austin, Texas

Copyright © 1972 by Sweet Publishing Company.
All rights reserved. No part of this book may be reproduced
by any means without permission in writing from the publisher, except for brief quotations embodied in critical articles,
or reviews.
Reprinted 1975

LIBRARY OF CONGRESS CATALOG CARD NUMBER: 72-77838

STANDARD BOOK NUMBER: 8344-0067-7

PRINTED IN U.S.A.

Acknowledgment

This commentary is based on the text of the Revised Standard
Version of the Bible, copyrighted 1946 and 1952 by the Division of Christian Education, National Council of Churches,
and used by permission.

Writers in *The Living Word Commentary* series have been
given freedom to develop their own understanding of the biblical text. As long as a fair statement is given to alternative
interpretations, each writer has been permitted to state his
own conclusions. Beyond the general editorial policies, the
editors have sought no artificial uniformity, and differences
are allowed free expression. A writer is responsible for his
contribution alone, and the views expressed are not necessarily the views of the editors or publisher.

Contents

I. INTRODUCTION   7
   The Author   7
   Date and Place of Writing   9
   Sources   10
   Purpose   12
   Special Studies   19
   Outline of Luke   21
   Selected Bibliography   21

II. THE PROLOGUE, 1:1-4   22

III. PREPARATION FOR JESUS' MINISTRY, 1:5—4:13   25
   Birth and Childhood of John and Jesus, 1:5—2:52   25
   John's Ministry, 3:1-20   67
   Inauguration and Preparation, 3:21—4:13   75

IV. THE GALILEAN MINISTRY, 4:14—9:50   84
   The Early Ministry, 4:14—6:11   84
   The Middle Ministry, 6:12—8:56   113
   The Galilean Ministry Completed, 9:1-50   151

I

Introduction

THE THIRD GOSPEL is generally regarded as a literary masterpiece among New Testament books. Here one finds some of the finest Greek in the New Testament, as well as many words unique to this book. A comparative study with Matthew and Mark reveals much material which would be lost had not this gospel preserved it. Even in the English text one is captured by the style of the author, including, for example, his unforgettable character portrayals. Truly he was a painter — with words.

THE AUTHOR

Arguments Favoring Luke

Though there were previous citations from and references to the gospel, extant sources ascribing it to Luke are not found until about A.D. 180, with Irenaeus (*Against Heresies* III, 1, 14), the Muratorian Canon, and the Anti-Marcionite Prologues. Following A.D. 180 there was widespread, unbroken, and apparently unchallenged tradition in favor of Luke as the author (cf. Clement of Alexandria, *Miscellanies* I, 21; Tertullian, *Against Marcion* IV,2; Eusebius, *Church History* III, xxiv, 5). If the gospel had been falsely credited to anyone other than its real author, it would not

INTRODUCTION

have been anyone as insignificant as Luke. It would far more likely have been attached to an apostle or other prominent figure in the early church. Luke, after all, is only casually named in three New Testament references (Col. 4:14; Phile. 24; 2 Tim. 4:11).

Though the book itself is anonymous, the New Testament supports and augments the traditional evidence, largely by a process of elimination. The author also wrote Acts, as can be discerned by comparing the introduction, language, style, and emphasis of the two books; or, more simply, by reading the last chapter of the third gospel and the first of Acts consecutively. Further, the author was Paul's companion at various stages in his travels, as the first person plural in Acts 16:10-17; 20:5—21:17; and 27:2—28:16 indicates.

It is presumed the author would not speak of himself in the third person, so everyone in the gospel and Acts who is so described can be eliminated. Luke 1:1-4 indicates he was not an eyewitness of Christ, so this omits others. Additionally, the author was with Paul in Rome (Acts 27:2), and this further narrows the field. By sifting the evidence one arrives at Luke as the best possibility. He is not mentioned in the gospel or Acts in the third person; it is reasonable to presume he was not an eyewitness of Jesus' life; and he was at Rome during Paul's imprisonment (Col. 4:14; Phile. 24).

Other evidence has also been adduced to support the Lukan thesis. Luke was a physician (Col. 4:4), and W. K. Hobart (*The Medical Language of St. Luke*, 1882) argued that the third gospel and Acts reflect a medical vocabulary. H. J. Cadbury, however, has challenged this evidence, arguing that the terminology is no different from that which any educated person of the day would use. Doubtless Hobart's case was overstated, but there still appear occasional evidences in the gospel of medical interest (for example, see 4:38, where Luke has "high fever," compared to the simple "fever" of Mark 1:30; or Luke 8:43, as compared to the semi-disparaging remark regarding doctors in Mark 5:26). These cases serve as corroboration to the other evidences for Lukan authorship.

The Man Luke

Colossians 4:10-14 differentiates Luke from the "men of the circumcision." This distinction is generally taken to indicate Luke was a Gentile, though Ellis, among others, dissents (see his commentary, pp. 52-55). Ellis sees Luke as a Hellenistic Jew and suggests he may be the same as the Lucius of Romans 16:21, who is identified as Paul's "kinsman." Second Timothy 4:11 shows Luke was in Rome during Paul's imprisonment, and Philemon 24 identifies him as Paul's fellow-worker.

It is also speculated that Luke may have been a Christian with the gift of prophecy. He shows an interest in prophecy and prophets, and E. C. Selwyn (*Expositor*, 7, 1909, 552f.) sees a prophetic style of writing in Acts 1-12.

The most prominent guesses have suggested Antioch of Syria or Philippi as his home. Another surmise is that he was a convert of Paul. The Anti-Marcionite Prologues, a doubtful authority, say he never married and that he died at the age of seventy-four. Another tradition says he was a painter.

DATE AND PLACE OF WRITING

It is impossible to determine conclusively when Luke was written. It was apparently before Acts, but that date is equally difficult to fix. One supposition is that Acts ends abruptly, without discussing the trial of Paul, because it was written before the latter event, i.e., in the early sixties. Luke would be dated just before this.

Many scholars, however, date the gospel in the early seventies. Interestingly, arguments for both the early and later dates are made from the relation of the gospel to the destruction of Jerusalem. Those contending for the sixties affirm that Luke, with his special interest in prophecy, would have clearly indicated that Jerusalem had fallen, had the

INTRODUCTION

event already occurred. On the other hand, those in favor of the seventies so argue on the basis of the comparison of Luke's apocalyptic discourse (chap. 21) with Mark 13. They point out Luke's greater specificity in describing the city's fall, which would indicate the event was past. Inasmuch as the gospel writers were not always giving the exact words of Jesus, it is possible that Jesus' words could have been reported by Luke in terms of the actual event. It does not seem possible, however, to arrive at a conclusive date for the gospel from this line of evidence.

Luke notes that other gospels had been written prior to his (1:1-4). There is good reason to believe one of these was Mark and that it was one of Luke's sources—see discussion below, and consult R. G. V. Tasker, *The Nature and Purpose of the Gospels* (Richmond:John Knox, 1962), or G. E. Ladd, *The New Testament and Criticism* (Grand Rapids: Eerdmans, 1967), or Ellis, pp. 21-30. If the date of Mark could be set, it would give a limit before which Luke would not have been written. However, the date of Mark is also uncertain, though a good suggestion is the late sixties.

Other considerations for dating Luke are inconclusive, so that the date of the book must remain uncertain.

Also unsure are the place of writing and destination of the book. It is assumed it was written for those living in the author's locale. It appears not to have been Palestine, since the way Palestinian place names are used implies the readers were unfamiliar with the country (see 1:26; 2:4; 4:31; 8:26; 13:51; and 24:13). Suggestions have included Rome, Achaia (Anti-Marcionite Prologues), and Asia Minor.

SOURCES

Luke's Research

From whence did the information come which comprises this remarkable work? Luke obviously had at his disposal material which the other gospel writers did not have or did

Luke's Sources

not choose to use. Almost a third of the gospel is peculiar to Luke, including six miracles, eighteen parables, and a great deal of discourse material.

Luke's prologue (1:1-4) indicates his careful research and use of sources. He almost certainly knew and relied on Mark, since about one-third of Luke is identical with Mark. This material makes up over half of the total content of Mark. Both Luke and Mark were with Paul in Rome (Col. 4:10, 14; Phile. 24) and doubtless were acquainted personally as well as literarily.

Besides Mark as a basic source, many close students of the Bible believe that a collection of the sayings of Jesus (called Q) may have been in circulation in the first century and that Luke and Matthew relied on it. It is obvious that Matthew and Luke give many sayings of Jesus not in Mark, and it is not unlikely that some collection, written or unwritten, lay behind this common material. Ellis suggests, that instead of a continuous source, there may have been a series of short Christian tracts containing tradition handed down from the Lord's lifetime that were the common possession of Matthew and Luke.

But beyond Mark and the material shared with Matthew, it is obvious that Luke had still other sources. He may have gained some information from Paul. One might also suppose Luke to have interviewed knowledgeable persons. His references to Mary's recollections (Luke 2:19, 51) might well indicate her. Other possibilities are Joanna (Luke 8:3) and Cleopas (Luke 24:18). He might have used the time Paul was imprisoned in Caesarea (Acts 23:23-26:32) to do research. In addition to special interviews, one must also consider the general knowledge Luke would gain in his life and travels as a Christian. Common material in Luke and John may imply yet another source. Other scholars suggest that original Hebrew material may lie behind the first two chapters, since they have a definite Semitic style. These sources furnished the information about what actually

INTRODUCTION

happened and about what Jesus taught. They were then employed by Luke for particular purposes.

Use of Sources

The four gospels do not always preserve Jesus' exact words. Although Jesus usually spoke Aramaic, as the survival of such Aramaic words as "mammon" (Matt. 6:24) and "abba" (Mark 5:41; 16:36) indicates, his teachings in the gospels have been transmitted in Greek. As any language student knows, there are different nuances of meaning involved in translating from one language to another. But there is a second consideration: the speeches of Jesus in any parallel printing of the gospels will show that in many cases the wording does not agree exactly. At best, then, only one account could have the Lord's *exact* words, whereas the others would contain the essence of them. It is possible also that all accounts may be to some extent a paraphrase of the original saying. These facts, to which the evidence points, do not mean the gospels are inaccurate or that any changes have been made which alter the central teachings. Indeed, the unique combination of variety and unity in the gospels provides multiple witness to the one divine reality which is Jesus Christ.

The question then is: Who or what was responsible for the changes, and why? Various reasons can be suggested. They may be the result of various local traditions. Or they could represent the changes of each writer, incorporated to fit his theological purpose. The needs of the community addressed in each work doubtless were significant in determining how the gospel was written.

PURPOSE

Uniqueness of Luke

In four gospels nothing is said about the almost thirty years of Jesus' life between infancy and baptism, except for an isolated instance when he was twelve. This indicates that a gospel does not record everything about Jesus' life, as a modern biography might. The gospels' literary form approximates proclamation rather than historical narrative. The gospels were written by those who believed in Jesus as the Christ, the Son of God. These men of faith were writing to produce or strengthen faith in others and not simply to tell the story for any factual interest it might bear. Consequently there is a sense in which a gospel is not completely understood unless the reader makes a personally positive response to it.

Matthew, Mark, and Luke were each led by God to portray the story of Jesus in a somewhat different way. Otherwise, the gospels would be identical, and hence only one would be necessary. Luke was writing for a particular audience (he names Theophilus), in a particular setting, with special emphases in mind. One can determine his special thrusts by noting material unique to his gospel, material found in the other gospels (especially Mark) which he omits, differences in his recording of events common to the other gospels, and how the outline of Luke differs from that of the other gospels. Since these differences do exist, they invite explanation. Probing them to discover the special thrust of Luke causes one to become increasingly appreciative of the skill with which the gospel was written.

Consideration of Luke's purpose must begin with 1:1-4. Here Luke sets forth his principles of research in which he engaged so he might "write an orderly account" that Theophilus might "know the truth concerning these things" of which he had been informed.

Special Emphases

Further specifics of Luke's purpose can be discovered by examining the special characteristics of the gospel. (To complete the picture, the inquiry must also be extended through Acts, since presumably both books had the same

INTRODUCTION

designs.) First, how does Luke show us Jesus? He is depicted as the perfect man, submissive to his parents, yet recognizing a prior relationship to God (2:40-52); he resists all temptation in his struggle with the devil (4:1-13) and even in his time of crucifixion is declared innocent by his antagonists (23:4, 14f., 20, 22, 27, 40-43, and 47).

Jesus' favorite title for himself was Son of man, which was probably messianic in nature (see discussion at 5:24). His role as Messiah was not political, as people had expected. The kingdom was a different sort of entity (see discussion of kingdom at 1:33). The title Son of God is probably also messianic in Luke (see discussion at 1:35). Note also the references to the word Christ (see discussion at 2:11).

Throughout the commentary, passages are marked with Roman numerals. These refer to collections of references in the introduction dealing with various themes. The picture of Jesus can be greatly enriched by noting the passages listed under I, which deal with the purpose of Jesus' mission on earth. His primary purpose was to effect man's salvation. The passages delineating this are collected under II.

Jesus is also presented frequently in the gospel as the one who knows human hearts (passages under III).

For a fuller listing of passages in which Luke depicts Jesus, consult the passages under IV.

. Jesus' true nature was concealed by his humanity, and it was only gradually that men came to know the secret of his true identity (note the development from 4:14-9:50). Scriptures dealing with this concept of secret and revelation are collected under V.

Finally, Luke demonstrates masterfully the reactions to Jesus during his ministry, offering a brilliant juxtaposition of acceptance and rejection as they represent the greater struggle between God and Satan (see discussion at 4:12; 10:18). These passages are compiled under VI.

Luke is also quite concerned about history as the stage on which the redemptive acts of God are presented. This

Luke's Emphases

involves the history of Israel, as well as setting the events into the larger context of the Roman world (see 2:1-3; 3:1). The gospel clearly shows God as the controller of history. There is great stress upon the fulfillment of God's purposes, whether expressed through the prophets, angels, John, Mary, Simeon, or Jesus himself. The passages showing this are collected under VII. Jesus operates under a sense of divine necessity, since God, not man, controls the events of his life (2:49; 9:22, 51; 12:50; 13:32f.; 18:31ff.; 22:22, 37, 42; 23:46; 24:7, 26, and 44).

The gospel also emphasizes the universality of the divine concern for mankind. It stresses the acceptability of the Gentile to God. Theophilus' name indicates he was a Gentile. Gentiles are specifically included in God's call (2:32; 24:47). The genealogy of Jesus is traced to Adam, the father of all humanity (3:23-38), rather than just to Abraham, father of Israel, as in Matthew.

No other gospel shows as much interest in the Samaritans as does Luke (9:51-56; 10:25-37; 17:11-19), and Jesus is seen as the one who cares for those whom others would despise. These include a sinful fisherman (5:8; 22:54-62; yet see 22:31f.; 24:34), a sinful woman, likely a prostitute (7:36-50), a detested tax collector (19:1-10), and a thief (23:39-43). Jesus speaks of God's desire to find and restore the lost (15:1-32; 19:1-10) and of a publican whose only plea before God was his confession of wretched sinfulness (18:9-14).

Luke's emphasis on the universality of the gospel is evident also in Jesus' concern for the poor, coupled with a clear depiction of the folly of trusting in riches (see discussion at 4:18; 6:24; and the passages collected under VIII). Luke also stresses the importance of women, an emphasis which was quite significant in that day prior to the emancipation of womanhood (see discussion at 1:5).

Luke's gospel also places considerable stress upon the Holy Spirit and upon prayer in Jesus' ministry (on the Holy Spirit, see discussion at 1:15; and on prayer, see discussions

INTRODUCTION

at 1:10, 13; 5:12). In addition to giving several of the teachings of Jesus on prayer which are not found elsewhere, Luke alone records that Jesus prayed at many important junctures of his life, such as his baptism, the great confession, the transfiguration, and the ascension. It is as if Luke is saying that God's action takes place in the power of the Holy Spirit, and that prayer is essential to spiritual success. There are other emphases in the gospel, which will be observed in reading through the commentary.

Were one among those for whom this gospel was initially written, he might better understand the foci of the work in terms of the community addressed. As it is, the reader can try to make educated guesses at the situation which called forth these particular emphases, and any others which he might discover. The challenge is open to the careful Bible student to continue searching to understand more fully why Luke wrote and what he especially wished to say.

Arrangement

The framework or outline of the gospel also can say something about the author's intent. At one time it was common to assume that the gospel accounts had to be strictly chronological to be historical. Comparative study and a better knowledge of the literary standards of the first century have shown it is no longer necessary to believe this. In the course of the commentary cases will be pointed out in which the order of events in Luke differs from that of the other gospels. Though one cannot give a definite solution in every case, it is logical to assume some reason for these alterations. Further study of them may be fruitful in indicating even more of Luke's intent.

Statements of Purpose

Some of the views taken by various scholars as to the basic purpose of Luke show how the gospel has been understood.

Luke's Purpose

1. The gospel was written to show the firm historical ground on which the faith of the Gentiles was based (1:1-4).

2. The alleged "apologetic purpose" of Luke-Acts sees in the books a determined attempt to demonstrate that there was nothing in Christianity to conflict with Roman law. Even though Jesus was crucified by Roman officials, and though the early church suffered at the hands of local magistrates (Acts 16), the upshot of each incident was that Christ and the Christians were innocent of any real breach of Roman law. It has been held that such material, which is more frequent in Acts, was intended to be used in defense of Paul at his trial before Nero.

3. Many Gentiles thought of Christianity as a Jewish sect (e.g., Gallio, Acts 18:12-17). Why then did the Jews come to reject it? One opinion has it that Luke was answering this question by showing that if Judaism were discredited, Christianity did not fall with it. In the same vein emphasis has been placed on Luke's picture of the church as the new, and real, Israel reliving the history of the old Israel. Thus, when Judaism goes, another Israel remains.

Whether or not this is a total rationale for Luke's writings, certainly it is one of his purposes. The point is well demonstrated by the way he treats the city of Jerusalem. In the Old Testament, besides being the religious and political center of Israel, the prophets also saw Jerusalem as the site of God's great blessings in the future — the messianic age (see, e.g., Isa. 40:1, 9-11; 44:28; 46:13; 52:8f.; 62:11f.). These same emphases are seen in Luke 1 and 2. Here the city is the center of Jewish piety, and reference is made to the consolation of Israel (2:25) and the redemption of Jerusalem (2:38) which the Jews anticipated. But as the book progresses the role of the city changes, and it becomes the place of opposition to Jesus (9:51; chs. 20-23). For rejecting its Messiah the city must be judged and will be destroyed (10:30; 13:4, 35; 19:27, 41-44; 21:5-36, esp. 20, 22, 23f.; 23:28). Yet it has a new future as the originating point of new Israel (24:49; Acts 1, 2). Thus the history of the city

INTRODUCTION

reflects the transition of the gospel to the Gentiles and the forming of a new people of God (see the references to Jerusalem at 2:22).

4. Conzelmann sees Luke as dividing redemptive history into three periods. The time of Israel ends with John the Baptist. The second period, fulfilling the first, is the life of Jesus. The last period is that of the church, extending from the ascension till the second coming. Conzelmann argues that the early church expected the imminent return of the Lord. When this did not occur, it was necessary for someone to rationalize the delay. This Luke did by taking the materials at his disposal and reworking them to push the Lord's return into the distant future. Conzelmann's work is careful and cannot be ignored. It is not, however, without objections. For one thing, the proposition that the church expected an imminent parousia is arguable. Further, it seems logical the early Christians would have the kind of faith that could accommodate a delayed return without needing a Luke to explain the non-occurrence of the event. Third, Conzelmann is rather skeptical as to the historical value of Luke. He seems to give some stories only symbolic value. Is it possible that a man writing within so few decades of the death of Jesus, considering the persistence of written and oral traditions about the Lord, could modify the basic material as radically without objection as Conzelmann's theory demands? Yet, the rejection of many of Conzelmann's positions still does not remove the necessity of seeing Luke as a "theologian of redemptive history."

Luke was both a historian (and an accurate one) and a theologian. Although his work as a theologian must be placed within the framework of God's oversight through the Spirit, yet within these bounds there is no doubt that he constructed his material in such a way as to make his own unique points. This commentary will try to note clues to the scheme of the author as they are discovered.

Luke's Themes

SPECIAL STUDIES

I. WHAT JESUS COMES TO DO (JESUS' MISSION). 1.32f., (68-75); 2:11, 31f.; (4:18f.), 43; 5:10, 20, 32; (6:20-23); 9:24; 10:20, 22; 12:8f., 51-53; 14:26f., 33; 18:18, 22, 30; 19:9f., 38, 42; 21:27f; 23:34, 42f.

II. FORGIVENESS AND SALVATION. 1:47, 68, 71, 77-79; 2:11, 30, 38; 3:3-14; 4:18; 5:20-24; 6:37; 7:43-50; 8:12-15; 9:24; 10:25-28; 11:4; 12:8-10; 13:3, 5, 23, 34; 14:14; 15:3-10, 24, 32; 19:9f.; 20:36; 21:19, 27f.; 23:34, 42f.; 24:21, 47.

III. JESUS KNOWING HEARTS (THOUGHTS). 4:23f.; 5:22, (27); 6:8; 7:40, 50; 8:45f.; 9:22, 47; 11:17, (39), (46ff.); 12:1, (54-56); 14:3, 5; 15:2f.; 16:15; 18:22; 19:5, 42; 20:3-8, 23, 46f.; 21:3f.; 22:31f., 34, (40, 46), 52f., 57-60; 23:9; 24:28, 38f.

IV. DEPICTION OF JESUS. 1:32f., 35, 43; 2:10f., 26, 34f., 46f., 51f.; 3:16f., 21f., 23-38; 4:3, 9, 14f., 16-21, 23f., 30, 32, 34-36, 39, 40-44; 5:3f., 10, 13f, 16f., 22; 11:20-22, 31f.; 12:8-10, 49f.; 13:32, 34; 14:26f., 33; 18:8, 31-33, 37-39; 19:38-40; 20:2, 8, 13-15, 17f., 41-44; 21:15, 27f., 36; 22:15-17, 27, (29f.), 37, 42, 67-71; 23:2f., 35, 37-39, 46; 24:5, 7, 19, 21, 26f., 39, 44, 46-49.

V. REVELATION AND SECRET. 1:13-17, 30-37, 41-43, 46-55, 67-79; 2:10-13, 15, 17, 26, 32, 35, 50; 3:2; 4:35, 41; 5:14f.; 8:8-10, 12, 16f., 39, 56; 9:2, 20f., 36, 45; 10:21f., 23f.; 12:2f., 10, 12, 56; 17:20f., 24; 18:34; 19:37-40; 20:2, 8, 41-44; 21:27f.; 22:16, 67-71; 23:2f., 5, 9; 24:11, 27, 30, 38-41, 45, 46-49.

VI. REACTIONS TO JESUS. 2:34f., 47f.; 3:19, 22; 4:2-13, 14f., 20, 22-24, 28f., 32, 34, 36, 37f., 40-42; 5:1, 5, 8-10, 11f., 15, 17-19, 21f., 25f., 28-30, 33; 6:2, 7, 11, 16f., 19, 22, 46, 47-49; 7:3f., 6-8, 11, 16f., 19f., 23, 31-35, 37f., 39, 44-46, 49; 8:1-3, 11-15, 17f., 19, 24f., 27f., 31, 33, 34-39, 40-44, 47, 49, 53, 56; 9:6-9, 11-13, 15, 19f., 22, 24, 26, 31, 33,

INTRODUCTION

36-38, 41, 43-45, 53, 57, 59, 61; 10:6-12, 13-15, 16f., 25, 39f.; 11:1, 14-16, 28f., 38, 51, 53f.; 12:1, 8-10, (47f.), 51-53; 13:13f., 17, 23, 25f., 28f., 31, 34; 14:4, 6, 15-24, 25; 15:1f.; 16:14; 17:5, 13-15, 20, 22-25, 30, 37; 18:11f., 14, 18, 23, 26, 28, 32f., 38f., 41, 43; 19:3, 6, 8, 16, 18, 20f., 37-39, 42, 47f.; 20:2, 7, 13-15, 17-22, 26, 27-33, 29f.; 21:7, 12-17, (22), (34), 38; 22:2, 3-6, 12, 21-23, 24, 28, 33, 38, 45, 47, 49f., 56-62, 63-65, 67f., 70f.; 23:1-5, 6-11, 14-16, 18-25, 26f., 31, 32-38, 39, 42, 47-49, 51-53, 55f.; 24:8f., 11, 14, 18-24, 26, 31-35, 39-42, 52f.

VII. PROPHECY AND FULFILLMENT:

From angels: 1:13-17, 20, 24, 31-35, 38, 45, 60-64; 2:21.

From Jesus: 6:21-23, 25, 35; 9:22, 26, 31, 44; 10:14f., 19; 11:9f., 13, 31f., 50f.; 12:2f., 40, 42-48, 49-53, 59; 13:3, 5, 24-30, 32, 35; 14:14; 16:9, 11f.; 18:20f., 22-37; 18:7f., 31-33; 19:26, 43f.; 20:34-36, 47; 21:6-9, 10-19, 20-24, 25-28, 31, 34-36; 22:16, 18, 21f., 29-32, 34, 61, 69; 23:28-31, 43; 24:6-8, 27, 44-47, 49.

From John: 3:16f.

From Mary: 1:48

From Old Testament: 1:54f., 67-79; 3:4-6; 4:10f., 18f., 21; 7:19-23, 27; 10:24; 18:31-33; 20:17f.; 20:41-44; 22:37; 24:25-27, 44-47.

From Simeon: 2:26, 29-31, 44-47.

VIII. MATERIAL THINGS. 1:52f.; 2:24; 3:11-14; 4:2-13, 18; 5:28; 6:20-22, 25, 30, 34, 35, 37; 7:22; 8:3, 14; 9:3; 10:4, 7; 11:40; 12:13-21, 22-31, 32-34; 1f:13f., 21f.; 15:11-17, 31; 16:1-9, 10-13, 14f., 19-31; 18:18-30; 19:1-10, 13-26; 21:1-4; 23:34.

OUTLINE OF LUKE

I. PROLOGUE, 1:1-4
II. PREPARATION FOR JESUS' MINISTRY, 1:5—4:13
   A. Birth and Childhood of John and Jesus, 1:5—2:52
   B. John's Ministry, 3:1-20
   C. The response of Jesus: Inauguration and Preparation, 3:21—4:13
III. THE GALILEAN MINISTRY, 4:14—9:50
   A. The Early Ministry: Acceptance and Rejection, 4:14—6:11
   B. The Middle Ministry, 6:12—8:56
   C. The Galilean Ministry Completed, 9:1-50
IV. THE JOURNEY TO JERUSALEM, 9:51—19:27
   A. The First Cycle, 9:51—13:30
   B. The Second Cycle, 13:31—17:10
   C. The Third Cycle, 17:11—19:27
V. THE MINISTRY IN JERUSALEM, 19:28—23:56
   A. The Public Ministry in Jerusalem, 19:28—21:38
   B. The Passion in Jerusalem, 22:1—23:56
VI. THE RESURRECTION AND ASCENSION, 24:1-53

SELECTED BIBLIOGRAPHY

CAIRD, G. B. *The Gospel of St. Luke.* Pelican Gospel Commentaries. Baltimore: Penguin, 1963.

CONZELMANN, HANS. *The Theology of St. Luke.* New York: Harper, 1961.

ELLIS, E. EARLE. *The Gospel of Luke.* The Century Bible, New Edition. London: Nelson, 1966.

GELDENHUYS, NORVAL. *Commentary on the Gospel of Luke.* The New International Commentary. Grand Rapids: Eerdmans, 1951.

MILLER, DONALD G. *The Gospel According to Luke.* The Layman's Bible Commentary. Richmond: John Knox, 1959.

PLUMMER, ALFRED. *A Critical and Exegetical Commentary on the Gospel According to St. Luke.* International Critical Commentary. Edinburgh: T & T Clark, 1906.

II

The Prologue, 1:1—4

LIKE MANY AUTHORS of his time, Luke opens with a formal introduction and in so doing provides the finest example of Greek within the New Testament. The remainder of the first two chapters is in a Hebraic style. Luke is the only gospel writer to enunciate his principles of composition so clearly. He deals with what Jesus "began" to do and teach (Acts 1:1), as in Acts he treats the continuation of the Lord's deeds and actions through the church.

[1] The identity of these **many** compilers is not known but they could include the "eyewitnesses" of verse 2. Likel Mark, and perhaps Matthew, may have been among them. The **many** almost certainly provided Luke with much material, which he supplemented by his own independent research (vs. 3). **Among us** shows Luke wrote from the viewpoint of the Christian community.

[2] The transmission of the message of Christ was rooted in personal experience (John 15:27; Acts 10:39; Heb. 2:3) which the church felt a strong need to maintain, as indicated by the qualification demanded of a prospective apostle (Acts 1:21f.). The materials about Jesus were probably first transmitted orally and later written, though oral and written materials would continue to circulate concurrently.

Theophilus LUKE 1:3

¹ Inasmuch as many have undertaken to compile a narrative of the things which have been accomplished among us, ²just as they were delivered to us by those who from the beginning were eyewitnesses and ministers of the word, ³it seemed good to me also, having followed all things closely *ᵃ* for some time past, to write an orderly account for you, most excellent Theophilus.

ᵃ Or accurately

---

[3] Luke had decided to join the "many" of verse 1, as indicated by his statement **it seemed good to me**. He was a careful researcher, having been so occupied **for some time past**—an early reference to Christian scholarship. Just as it does a disservice to the Bible to deny the divine element in its writing, it also does a disservice to deny the personal initiative of the particular author. God's guidance also operated in the collecting and using of his material by the evangelist.

It is impossible to know the exact import of **orderly**, but it need not imply a criticism of the other narratives. The term is peculiar to Luke in the New Testament (Luke 8:1; Acts 3:24; 11:4; 18:23) and merely implies an arrangement of some sort, whether temporal, spatial, or logical.

Theophilus (see Acts 1:1), a common name, means "friend of God." **Most excellent** was often used of a person of rank (Acts 23:26; 24:3; 26:25). The formality of the title might indicate that he was not a brother in Christ, though some think **Theophilus** was a pseudonym used to protect an influential Christian from discrimination. Yet, though he had been "informed" regarding the faith, his actual religious profession must remain in doubt. It has been suggested that he was Luke's patron. Perhaps he represented cultured Gentiles whom Luke wished to reach. Others think the name was meant to describe a class, but this is unlikely in view of the specificity of Luke's language. An individual dedication did not rule out the intention of the work for a wider audience. In fact, it marked a work for publication.

LUKE 1:4 — *Certainty*

⁴that you may know the truth concerning the things of which you have been informed.

---

[4] If this verse implies Theophilus had gained erroneous information from the other sources available to him, then misleading information about Jesus was circulating rather early. Yet the expression may simply refer to more solid grounding in Christian teaching, with no depreciatory implications regarding other narratives. Luke may have felt that his readers were in need of stronger support for their knowledge of the Lord (see John 20:31). Here was to be a solid and systematic treatment of materials previously known in a partial and more scattered manner.

Informed comes from the Greek word "catechized," though not carrying the implications which the word came to have in later religious practice.

III

Preparation for Jesus' Ministry, 1:5 — 4:13

BIRTH AND CHILDHOOD OF JOHN AND JESUS, 1:5 — 2:52

THIS SECTION pictures the end of the age of the prophets as it moves toward the time of Christ. The pertinent events are enacted by the power of God—a theme throughout the Lukan writings (1:13, 19, 25, 26, 31, 35, 37, 38, 41, 58, 66, 67; 2:9, 13f., 15, 25-27, 36). Emphasis is placed on God's promises, either as they are fulfilled or as they are yet to find consummation (1:13-17, 20, 24, 31-33, 35, 36, 45, 48, 50-55, 57, 68-79; 2:5, 10, 11f., 21, 26-32, 34f., 38; see VII). It is in the poetic parts of these chapters that the theme of God's actions is most clearly specified. They form the heart of the section.

Those through whom God works and who are most receptive to his good news are the pious in Israel. There is stress on the devout religious life of the main characters (1:6, 38, 45, 59; 2:22ff., 25-27, 36f., 39, 40). It is in this pattern that one sees the first self-consciousness of Jesus

[5] In the days of Herod, king of Judea, there was a priest named Zechariah,[b] of the division of Abijah; and he had a wife of the daughters of Aaron, and her name was Elizabeth.

[b] Greek *Zacharias*

(2:49). The people receptive to God are often among the unimportant people in the land, such as Mary or the shepherds (see discussion of the poor, 4:18).

In contrast to the prologue and the rest of the book, this section is markedly Hebraic in tone. Old Testament references abound, and the style may be in conscious imitation of the Septuagint.

The Promise of John's Birth, 1:5-25

[5] **Herod** the Great (37 B.C.-A.D. 4) ruled all of Palestine, which is what **Judea** in this verse means (see 7:17; 23:5; Acts 2:9; 10:37; and cf. Luke 4:44). He was an Idumaean who adopted the Jewish religion and who depended on Rome for his sovereignty. He was the ancestor of that line of Herods met so often in the New Testament and would certainly have been well known to Luke's Gentile readers (see vol. 1 of this series, *The World of the New Testament*, pp. 58-60). Thus Luke anchored his story in the political situation of the time.

By contrast to **Herod**, the story centers on a **priest** and his **wife, Zechariah** and **Elizabeth**. The names mean, respectively, "remembered by Yahweh" (Jehovah), and "God is my oath," or "my God is an oath." **The division of Abijah** was one of the twenty-four groups of priests (1 Chron. 23:6; 24:10; 28:13), each of which served at the temple for one week twice a year (see 1 Chron. 24:19; 2 Chron. 8:14; 23:8; 31:2; Neh. 12:4, 17). Specific regulations required **a priest** to marry a virgin of his own people (Lev. 21:13-15). It was a double distinction for **Zechariah** to be **a priest** and married to a priest's daughter.

Mention of **Elizabeth** is the first instance of a special emphasis on women which characterizes the gospel (see introduction). The word for woman (*gunē*) is unique to Luke

Childlessness LUKE 1:6-9

⁶And they were both righteous before God, walking in all the commandments and ordinances of the Lord blameless. ⁷But they had no child, because Elizabeth was barren, and both were advanced in years.

⁸Now while he was serving as priest before God when his division was on duty, ⁹according to the custom of the priesthood, it fell to him by lot to enter the temple of the Lord and burn incense.

---

in 1:5, 13, 18, 24, 28, 42; 4:26; 7:28, 37, 39, 44, 50; 8:2, 3; 10:38; 11:27; 13:11, 12; 14:20, 26; 15:8; 17:32; and 18:29.

[6] The character of Zechariah and Elizabeth showed them ready to be used by God. One tribute to their goodness was the absence of bitterness at Elizabeth's barrenness, in spite of how intensely they must have wanted children. The Greek term here translated **righteous** is found in Luke at 1:6, 17; 2:25; 5:32; 12:57; 14:14; 15:7; 18:9; 20:20; 23:47, 50; and in Acts 3:14; 4:19; 7:52; 10:22; 22:14; and 24:15.

[7] Since absence of children was a sign of God's disfavor, the Jews attached great importance to having offspring (Lev. 20:20f.; 1 Sam. 1:11; 2 Sam. 6:23; Ps. 127:3-6; 128:3; Jer. 22:30). In this case the contrast of the barrenness and the goodness of the couple was unusual. A man lived on in his descendants, and to die childless was to be "blotted out of Israel" (Deut. 25:5f.). One can imagine how **Elizabeth** would be the subject of discussion among her acquaintances. Her childlessness continues the pattern of the **barren** woman found through the Old Testament (Sarah, Rebekah, Rachel, Samson's mother, and Hannah). The point of the narrative in these instances was to show the greatness of God's power, for when a **barren** woman (especially if past the age of childbearing) became pregnant, there was no doubt the matter was made possible by God. Thus he acted graciously to bless his people.

[8, 9] Priestly service involved the duties of the maintenance of the temple and observation of the rituals of worship. Originally only the high priest was to offer **incense** (Ex.

LUKE 1:10, 11 — *Prayer*

¹⁰ And the whole multitude of the people were praying outside at the hour of incense. ¹¹ And there appeared to him an angel of the Lord standing on the right side of the altar of incense.

30:7f.), but apparently others came to be allowed to do so. The honor was restricted to once in a lifetime for any priest, and at that many never had the privilege. Because of the chance (or providence, cf. Acts 1:26) of the lot, Zechariah was placed in a most auspicious position for the momentous events to follow. As God was praised, he revealed his will.

[10] Fire was taken from the outside altar, and the priest awaited the signal to kindle it upon the **incense** altar, which was located in the Holy Place just in front of the curtain separating it from the Most Holy Place. When the smoke of the **incense** ascended, the people prostrated themselves in silent prayer, usually of several minutes duration (on burning of **incense** connected with prayer, see Ps. 141:2; Rev. 5:8 and 8:3f.).

This is Luke's first mention of prayer. The word used here (*proseuchomai*) is found also in 3:21; 5:16; 6:12, 28; 9:18, 28, 29; 11:1f. (cf. also 3-11); 18:1, 10, 11; 20:47; 22:40f., 44, 46; Acts 1:24; 6:6; 8:15; 9:11, 40; 10:9, 30; 11:5; 12:12; 13:3; 14:23; 16:25; 20:36; 21:5; 22:17; 28:8. In addition to this word, Luke also employs others (cf. notes at 1:13; 5:12 and the introduction).

The Greek term for **multitude** (*plēthos*) is used twenty-five times by Luke, and is found only seven times in the rest of the New Testament (in the gospel the term is found at 2:13; 5:6; 6:17; 8:37; 19:37; 23:1 and 27).

[11] In Acts 10:3 Luke also depicts an angelic response to prayer. **Angel** can also mean "messenger." This was angels' main role, especially in the gospels. The concept is found throughout the Old Testament, and the manifestation, though frightening when endured by Zechariah personally, was well known to his theology (see on angels 1:13, 18, 19, 26, 28, 30, 34, 35, 38; 2:9, 10, 13, 15, 21; 4:10; 9:26; 12:8f.; 15:10; 16:22; 22:43; and 24:23). **The right side of the**

Prayer Answered   LUKE 1:12, 13

[12] And Zechariah was troubled when he saw him, and fear fell upon him. [13] But the angel said to him, "Do not be afraid, Zechariah, for your prayer is heard, and your wife Elizabeth will bear you a son, and you shall call his name John.

---

altar was the place of honor. For a similar instance to this, see Daniel 9:20-23.

[12] Here are seen both the profound awe, and the irresistible attraction, which man feels in the presence of the divine. Luke frequently notes the fearful reaction of men to God's acts (1:29f., 65; 2:9f.; 5:8, 26; 7:16; 8:25, 35, 37; 9:34, 45; 21:26; 24:37; Acts 2:43; 5:5, 11; 10:4; 19:17). The emotion would be a combination of fright and reverence.

[13] **Do not be afraid** is an expression found also in Luke 1:30; 2:10; 8:50; 12:4f., 7, 32; Acts 18:9; 27:24. The reassurance was to indicate that God's purposes were for good, not harm. See Genesis 17:19; Daniel 10:12; and Acts 10:31, where similar language is found.

Zechariah's prayer may have been the one offered as the incense was burned, which likely would be for the redemption of Israel and the coming of the messianic kingdom. John's birth was, in part, an answer to that. But more probably it was the couple's petition for a child. If they had continued to offer this **prayer,** after years of childlessness and with advancing old age, their persistence was a great testimony to their faith. Yet even the strongest faith may waver, as did Zechariah's shortly.

Perhaps it was God's will to defer his answer until such time as it would be a clear and undeniable demonstration of his power and mercy. Certainly the answer bore special significance to have come so auspiciously. Luke would be careful to record these words, for they help build his special case regarding **prayer** and its power. The word for **prayer** here is *deēsis* and is found also in 2:37 and 5:33 (see 1:10 and the introduction).

That **Elizabeth** would **bear** a child was the first of a series of staggering announcements. It was followed by further

LUKE 1:14, 15 — *Joy*

¹⁴**And you will have joy and gladness,
and many will rejoice at his birth;**
¹⁵**for he will be great before the Lord,
and he shall drink no wine nor strong drink,
and he will be filled with the Holy Spirit,
even from his mother's womb.**

---

impressive specifics. **John** means "God's gift" or "God is gracious." The later insistence on the name (1:60-63) demonstrated its special significance. It was, and would continue to be, a sign of God's special action. Many people were named **John,** but the meaning of this child's name would be more impressive when the circumstances under which it was given were known.

[14] This verse first gives the reaction of the parents, to be followed by that of a broader circle. **Joy** *(chara)* is found eight times in the gospel (2:10; 8:13; 10:17; 15:7, 10; 24:41, 52), and every instance except one (8:13) is unique to Luke. All are descriptive of the joy in heaven and on earth caused by what God does in Christ. **Gladness** means extreme joy or exultation and is found elsewhere in the New Testament only in Luke 1:44; Acts 2:46; Hebrews 1:9; and Jude 24. The term, with its cognates, implies the salvation which God brings and which produces such extreme rejoicing. It signifies the joy of those within the community of the last time, i.e., the kingdom of God. **Rejoice** *(chairō)* is frequently used by Luke to describe reactions to the blessings of the Messiah (6:23; 10:20; 15:5, 32; 19:6, 37; and possibly 1:28). The idea of joy finds a significant place in the Lucan writings. Compare also "rejoice with," 1:58.

Not only his parents, but **many** would be beneficiaries of the divine action which John's ministry would inaugurate. The text emphasizes God's intention to promote man's well-being.

[15] Here are several parallels to the story of Samuel (1 Sam. 1, 2), which are made even more significant by

Holy Spirit   LUKE 1:15, 16

¹⁶ **And he will turn many of the sons of Israel to the Lord their God,**

---

the similarity of the song of Mary in verses 46-55 to that of Hannah in First Samuel 2:1-10.

Abstinence from **wine** and **strong drink** may refer to the Nazirite vow (Num. 6:2-21, esp. 2-8; Judges 13:4f., 7; 16:17; 1 Sam. 1:11; see also Lev. 10:9 for prohibition of **wine** for priests). However, some facets of that vow are not specified here (e.g., allowing the hair to grow). Thus the idea may be simply that the child was consecrated to God, and instead of the stimulant of strong drink he would have that of the **Holy Spirit** (see 5:33; 7:33; and cf. Eph. 5:18).

This is the first of many Lukan references to the **Holy Spirit**. The **Spirit** is mentioned only five times in Matthew, four times each in Mark and John, but seventeen times in Luke, and over fifty times in Acts (Luke 1:35, 41, 67; 2:25ff.; 3:16, 22; 4:1, 14, 18; 10:21; 11:13; 12:10, 12; and with 24:49 cf. Acts 1:2, 8). Luke clearly indicates that by this power the great constitutive events of the Christian faith took place, and their meaning was revealed (1:41, 67; 2:25-27). All of these cases of the Spirit's action formed a sign of the arrival of the messianic age, according to Jewish expectations (see Isa. 32:15; Ezek. 11:19; 36:26; Joel 2:28ff.).

Spirit possession from **his mother's womb** probably refers to the permanence of John's filling. Often in the Old Testament a prophet was temporarily inspired or guided by God. John would exceed them (see 7:28). This is the only reference specifically ascribing **the Spirit** to John, but it comprehends his entire ministry. Thus, his later activity as the preacher of repentance and herald of the Messiah offers the best commentary on the role of this gift. His **Spirit**-filled ministry made him a sign of the last days.

[16, 17] John's work is depicted in terms of the prophet **Elijah**, as he was described in Malachi 4:5f. (see also Mal. 3:1). Ecclesiasticus 48:9f., probably under the influence of

> ¹⁷ and he will go before him in the spirit and power of Elijah,
> to turn the hearts of the fathers to the children,
> and the disobedient to the wisdom of the just,
> to make ready for the Lord a people prepared."
> ¹⁸ And Zechariah said to the angel, "How shall I know this? For I am an old man, and my wife is advanced in years."

Malachi, exhibits similar language. Though the identification of **Elijah** and John is not as explicit as in Matthew 11:14 and 17:10-13, Luke does present the Baptist as the Elijah-like restorer who would stimulate a time of repentance to precede the Messiah's coming. John's rustic life-style bore remarkable similarities to that of **Elijah**. See other **Elijah** references in 4:25f.; 9:8, 19, 30, 33.

Not only would Zechariah become a father, but the child's sex, name, character, endowments, and mission were specified. Each of these pyramided on the other to increase the marvel, and it is understandable how the old man's faith could have been severely tested by the angelic announcement.

Power (*dunamis*) is a word found often in Luke (1:35;4:14, 36; 5:17; 6:19; 8:46; 9:1; 10:13, 19; 19:37; 21:26f.; 22:69; 24:49; Acts 1:8; 2:22; 3:12; 4:7, 33; 6:8; 8:10, 13; 10:38; 19:11). In the gospel it refers in every case but one (21:26) to the **power** of God. In several cases it is closely connected with the work of the Holy Spirit (1:17; 1:35; 4:14; 24:49; and cf. Acts 1:8). Many of the gospel references are to Jesus' works, which are messianic signs accomplished in the **power** of the Spirit (4:18f.).

[18] Zechariah would soon enough know if Elizabeth were going to conceive, but he may have been so startled that he wanted immediate confirmation. He even gave reasons why he believed the angel must be wrong (for similar reactions, see Gen. 15:8; 17:17; 18:12; Ex. 4:1; Judges 6:17, 36-40; 2 Kings 20:8; and Isa. 38:22; cf. Isa. 7:11; 38:7; 1 Cor. 1:22; and Rom. 4:19-21).

Good News   LUKE 1:19, 20

[19] And the angel answered him, "I am Gabriel, who stand in the presence of God; and I was sent to speak to you, and to bring you this good news. [20] And behold, you will be silent and unable to speak until the day that these things come to pass, because you did not believe my words, which will be fulfilled in their time."

---

[19] The **angel** and the message were sign enough to Zechariah. When he said "**I am** . . . **old**," **Gabriel** answered with another **I am,** offering a sharp contrast between human uncertainty and divine assurance. **Gabriel** means "man of God," or "God has shown himself mighty." Daniel 8:16 and 9:21f. picture him as a revealer. The Pseudepigrapha show him as an intercessor (1 Enoch 9:1; 40:6; 2 Enoch 21:3) and as a destroyer (1 Enoch 9:9f.; 54:6). The New Testament pictures him as a revealer and bringer of assurance (Luke 1:11-20, 26-38; cf. Heb. 1:14).

Bring good news in its other uses in the gospel (2:10; 3:18; 4:18, 43; 7:22; 8:1; 9:6; 16:16; 20:1) always refers to the message about and of Jesus. It was a sign of his messiahship (7:22), which was inspired by the Spirit (4:18). The **good news** was specifically identified as the coming of the kingdom (4:43; 16:16; cf. discussion at 1:33). In fact in 16:16 the preaching of **good news** is the mark of the age of Jesus, which was proclaimed since John. To the readers of Luke, from their vantage point of several decades of Christian history and their more complete knowledge of Christ, the term would have rich meaning, whatever it implied to Zechariah.

[20] Zechariah's affliction would be a "sign" to him and to others, so that his request was **fulfilled** through this misfortune. If he were tempted to waver again, his speechlessness served as a reminder. He had received such wonderful news, and now he would be unable to communicate it freely as he wished (on dumbness see Ezek. 3:26f. and Dan. 10:15).

LUKE 1:21-23   *Wonder*

21 And the people were waiting for Zechariah, and they wondered at his delay in the temple. 22 And when he came out, he could not speak to them, and they perceived that he had seen a vision in the temple; and he made signs to them and remained dumb. 23 And when his time of service was ended, he went to his home.

Luke notes other dire consequences that came upon people who doubted God (Acts 5:5; 13:11).

The **things** to **come to pass** apparently referred to the birth of the child, for it was shortly thereafter that Zechariah spoke again (1:64). Since his healing was now involved, Zechariah would be doubly anxious for fulfillment of Gabriel's message. (VII)

[21] According to the Talmud the priest, to prevent anxiety, would come out of **the temple** as soon as possible, since some traditions held that in the Holy Place one might incur the divine displeasure and be slain (Lev. 16:13). Also it was customary after the evening burning of incense (if this were the evening occasion) for the priest to come out and bless the people. Zechariah's absence, for these reasons, and because **the people** knew that his duties did not take long, puzzled them. The word for **wondered** is a favorite one of Luke (1:63; 2:18, 33; 4:22; 7:9; 8:25; 9:43; 11:14, 38; 20:26; 24:12, 41; Acts 2:7; 3:12; 4:13; 7:31;13:41). It is generally used in the gospel to describe reactions to Jesus.

[22] When Zechariah's dumbness became evident, the people would want information, which would both increase his frustration and begin building his faith. It was probably by some improvised sign language that they knew of the vision. There is no indication he told them the content of the message, and it would have been most difficult unless he had written it out at once. Nor may they have been aware there was a message at all.

[23] **Service** *(leitourgein)* in biblical Greek refers to priestly **service** in the worship of God and also to **service** for the needy. From the word comes the English "liturgy."

Mary   LUKE 1:24-27

[24] After these days his wife Elizabeth conceived, and for five months she hid herself, saying, [25] "Thus the Lord has done to me in the days when he looked on me, to take away my reproach among men."

[26] In the sixth month the angel Gabriel was sent from God to a city of Galilee named Nazareth, [27] to a virgin betrothed to a man whose name was Joseph, of the house of David; and the virgin's name was Mary.

[24, 25] Elizabeth's exultant statement is another example of the joy God's acts would bring (see 1:14). Her reproach was her barrenness, not some flaw in her character for which God was punishing her (see Gen. 30:23; 1 Sam. 1:5-8; 2 Sam. 6:23; Hos. 9:11; cf. especially Hannah's prayer in 1 Sam. 1:11).

The Annunciation to Mary, 1:26-38 (Matt. 1:18-25)

[26] **In the sixth month** (of Elizabeth's pregnancy) **Gabriel** came to a seemingly unimportant maiden in **Nazareth**. Thus Jesus and John were to be nearly the same age. The interval made it possible for Mary to be sure of Elizabeth's condition, thus confirming the validity of Gabriel's promises. Describing **Nazareth** as **a city of Galilee** indicates Luke may have been writing for people who were not familiar with the geography of Palestine.

[27] The choice of **Mary** was not one demanded by her merit (though she was of excellent character) but by God's grace. Luke's emphasis on her virginity stresses the supernatural character of what was to occur.

Betrothal usually lasted a year, during which time the woman lived with friends. Her property was vested in her future husband, and unfaithfulness during this period was punishable, like adultery, by death (Deut. 22:23f.). A betrothal was broken by divorce, and if the man died, the woman was considered a widow.

The Messiah would come from David's family (2 Sam. 7:12f.). But was **Joseph**, or **Mary**, of the house of David?

LUKE 1:28-31 — *Annunciation*

²⁸And he came to her and said, "Hail, O favored one, the Lord is with you!"ᶜ ²⁹But she was greatly troubled at the saying, and considered in her mind what sort of greeting this might be. ³⁰And the angel said to her, "Do not be afraid, Mary, for you have found favor with God. ³¹And behold, you will conceive in your womb and bear a son, and you shall call his name Jesus.

ᶜ Other ancient authorities add *"Blessed are you among women!"*

Joseph undoubtedly was (2:4), but some suppose **Mary** was of Levi, since she was related to Elizabeth (verse 36). But the relationship did not demand both women be of the same tribe. Verses 32 and 69, together with the fact that **Joseph** was not the real father, seem to indicate that **Mary** must also have been of Davidic descent.

[28] **Hail** is interpreted by some as meaning "rejoice" (see notes on 1:14), and some have felt **O favored one** might better be translated "endued with grace." **The Lord is with you** was not a report of Mary's nearness to God but of the special way in which he would intervene in her life (cf. Judges 6:12).

[29] Compare Mary's reaction (fear and curiosity) with Zechariah's in verse 12. **Troubled** is used nowhere else in the New Testament, and the word is stronger than that describing Zechariah's reaction. She probably **considered** why she should be approached in such a way or what message would follow such an auspicious greeting. The psychological detail Luke gives indicates he may have "interviewed" Mary, as later passages will confirm.

[30, 31] **The angel** reassured **Mary**, as he had Zechariah (verse 13), by reaffirming the concept of verse 28. As with John, not only was a birth foretold, but considerable detail was given about the child (sex, **name,** character, purpose, etc.; cf. Matt. 1:21-23). This verse is virtually a quotation of Isaiah 7:14 (which is quoted in Matt. 1:23), with "Immanuel" changed to **Jesus** (cf. also Gen. 16:11; Judges 13:3).

Son

³²He will be great, and will be called the Son of the Most High;
and the Lord God will give to him the throne of his father David,
³³and he will reign over the house of Jacob forever;
and of his kingdom there will be no end."

If Jesus means "Savior" (which some dispute), then even more than with John the name had special significance.

[32] **Most High** is used seven times in Luke (1:35, 76; 2:14; 6:35; 8:28; 19:38) and only four times in the rest of the New Testament.

The idea of divine sonship is repeated in the "Son of God" of verse 35. The concept of divine fatherhood was expressed several places in the Old Testament (Ex. 4:22; Jer. 31:20; Hos. 11:1) and was especially relevant to the Davidic king (2 Sam. 7:14; Ps. 2:7). But Jesus' life and teaching gave the concept greater breadth (see Mark 11:9f.), and consequently the church came to know the fatherhood of God in a way no Hebrew had previously enjoyed.

The child's reception of David's **throne** was an exciting concept, since the Jews had no king at the time. The statement invited reflection on the Old Testament promises. The Lord's act, then, involved more than just one woman and one child by embracing the entire complex of events that must come with the reestablishment of the kingdom. For references to Jesus' mission, see introduction, I; depiction of Jesus, see introduction, IV.

[33] **The house of Jacob**, as subsequent Christian history showed, was larger than just physical Israel. The eternal reign was in accord with the promise in 2 Samuel 7:14 (see also Dan. 2:44; 7:14; Mic. 4:7; Matt. 28:18-20; and Heb. 7:24).

This is Luke's first reference to **kingdom** (see 4:5, 43; 6:20; 7:28; 8:1, 10; 9:2, 11, 27, 60, 62; 10:9, 11; 11:2, 17,

LUKE 1:33-35 *Kingdom*

³⁴And Mary said to the angel, "How can this be, since I have no husband?" ³⁵And the angel said to her,
"The Holy Spirit will come upon you,
and the power of the Most High will overshadow you;
therefore the child to be born[d] will be called holy,
the Son of God.

[d] Other ancient authorities add *of you*

18, 20; 12:31, 32; 13:18, 20, 28, 29; 14:15; 16:16; 17:20, 21; 18:16, 17, 24, 25, 29; 19:11, 12, 15; 21:10, 31; 22:16, 18, 29, 30; 23:42, 51; Acts 1:3, 6; 8:12; 14:22; 19:8; 20:25; 28:23, 31). The **kingdom** message was the basic proclamation of Jesus' Galilean ministry (4:43; 8:1) and was that with which he commissioned the twelve (9:2) and the seventy (10:9, 11). In some cases Jesus spoke of the **kingdom** as yet future, though (often) imminent (cf. 9:27). On others it was present (at least germinally) already in his ministry (11:20; 16:16; 17:20f.—but see discussions at the references). Thus it would seem the ministry of Jesus was the inaugural to the **kingdom**—an entity which was to come in its fullest form at a future time (see Acts 1:6-8; 2:1-4). Association of the **kingdom** with the cross is implied in 22:16, 18. Jesus saw his death and resurrection as the fulfillment of his messianic mission, so the **kingdom** was a necessary corollary of that. For the sake of the **kingdom** the greatest devotion must be practiced (9:60, 62; 14:25-33; 18:24, 25, 29; 19:15). Specific **kingdom** blessings are indicated in 6:20; 7:28; 12:31; 13:28; 19:17, 19, 24, 26; 22:30; 23:42f.

[34] **Mary** did not, like Zechariah, seek a sign. But she did seek further information (cf. John 3:4, 9). Her statement was in the present tense, "I do not know a man," and in no sense implies the future and perpetual virginity of **Mary.**

[35] By this unprecedented statement Mary began to understand that God's direct power, and not normal union with a male, would make her conceive. On **Holy Spirit,** see 1:15; on **power,** see 1:17. **Overshadow** recalls the cloud

Son of God LUKE 1:35, 36

³⁶ And behold, your kinswoman Elizabeth in her old age has also conceived a son; and this is the sixth month with her who was called barren.

---

that overshadowed the tabernacle during the wilderness wandering. The word is also used in all the synoptic gospels of the cloud that came at the transfiguration. The only other usage in the New Testament is Acts 5:15. The term is always used of divine **power.** The concept is reminiscent of the **Spirit** hovering over the waters in Genesis 1:2. Here the **Spirit** would be active in a new "creation" of God.

The child would **be called holy, the Son of God,** because of the divine action in producing this union. To later Christians the term **holy,** when referred to their Lord, meant free from all taint. But Mary, at the time, probably only understood that **the child** would be consecrated in some way (see also Ex. 13:12; Isa. 43). Other usages of the term are in 1:49, 70, 72; 2:23; 4:34 and 9:26).

Son of God is reminiscent of Psalm 2:7; Isaiah 7:14 and 9:6. Though Christ seldom used it of himself (Matt. 27:43; John 10:36), it was used of him several times in the synoptic gospels (Matt. 4:3; 16:16; Mark 3:11; 5:7; and in Luke 3:22; 4:3, 9, 41; 8:28; 9:35; and 22:70). In Luke the expression refers to Jesus' messiahship. This can be seen especially by comparing this verse with 1:32f., 3:22 with 3:15; and 22:70 with 22:67-69. Also in Luke 4:41 the demons recognized Jesus as the Christ by calling him **Son of God.** In 4:9 the devil used Psalm 91, which the Jews interpreted messianically, in connection with the title **Son of God.** Note that in Luke 9:35 **the Son** is God's chosen, while in 23:35 the Messiah is God's chosen. Also compare Luke 2:49; 23:34, 46. It is in other parts of the New Testament that this title was used more particularly of Jesus' divine nature. (IV, VII)

[36] Elizabeth's condition would give Mary a sign she had not requested and reassure her regarding God's actions. Apparently Mary was previously unaware **Elizabeth** was

LUKE 1:37-39 *Mary's Faith*

³⁷ For with God nothing will be impossible." ³⁸ And Mary said, "Behold, I am the handmaid of the Lord; let it be to me according to your word." And the angel departed from her.

³⁹ In those days Mary arose and went with haste into the hill country, to a city of Judah,

---

pregnant. The exact nature of the kinship of the two women is unknown.

[37] This verse could also be translated, "from God no word shall be impossible." The difference in meaning is not great. The essence of this statement was also in the angelic word to Sarah in Genesis 18:14. There a chosen race was to be begun, and here a new humanity was anticipated. Further, Mary's child would be the ultimate fulfillment of the promise to Abraham. This verse is a key statement of the annunciation stories, as they chronicle the amazing actions of God (see Matt. 19:26; Mark 10:27; Luke 18:27). (V)

[38] A **handmaid** was a slave. The feminine form is found in the New Testament only here, 1:48, and Acts 2:18. **Mary** had heard startling news. She was risking a stoning if the law of Deuteronomy 22:23f. were followed. At least there was good possibility of a scandal when her pre-marital pregnancy became known. Her relations with Joseph, if he were not sympathetic, would be jeopardized. Yet she accepted her mission and thus (in contrast to Zechariah) showed herself a person of remarkable faith.

The text does not say when the moment of conception was, whether at this time or later. From Matthew 1:18-21 one can learn that she did not tell Joseph what had happened, since it was necessary for an **angel** to explain her pregnancy to him. (VII)

Mary's Visit to Elizabeth, 1:39-56

[39] Elizabeth's home town may have been Hebron, since many priests lived there. **Mary** no doubt **went** because of the words of Gabriel (verse 36) to share in her kinswoman's good fortune.

Elizabeth's Greeting   LUKE 1:40-45

[40] and she entered the house of Zechariah and greeted Elizabeth. [41] And when Elizabeth heard the greeting of Mary, the babe leaped in her womb; and Elizabeth was filled with the **Holy Spirit** [42] and she exclaimed with a loud cry, "Blessed are you among women, and blessed is the fruit of your womb! [43] And why is this granted me, that the mother of my Lord should come to me? [44] For behold, when the voice of your greeting came to my ears, the babe in my womb leaped for joy. [45] And blessed is she who believed that there would be[c] a fulfillment of what was spoken to her from the Lord."

_{Or *believed, for there will be*}

[40, 41] Luke, a physician, would know that an emotional experience of the mother would cause movement of the fetus. Here it was connected with her reception of the **Holy Spirit** (see notes at 1:15). It seemed a sign from God, in special recognition of God's great provisions for man through Mary. Because of the influence of the **Spirit**, **Elizabeth** spoke from sources beyond her own knowledge (cf. 1:67; 2:25-27; and 12:12).

[42] Elizabeth's exclamation was not unlike uncontrollable ecstatic behavior. Luke is fond of recording such strong expressions of emotion (2:10; 4:33; 8:28; 17:15; 19:36; 23:23, 46; 24:52). The nature of the words may imply that Mary had already conceived. See a similar circumstance in 11:27f. (on the blessing, cf. Deut. 28:4 and Judges 5:24). Approximately forty percent of the usages of the word **blessed** *(eulogeō)* are Lukan. Those cases in the gospel are 1:42, 64; 2:28, 34; 6:28; 9:16; 13:35; 19:38; 24:30; 50, 51, 53.

[43] **Lord** doubtless referred to the Messiah, since obviously it was not the Father (cf. 21:41-44), as in verse 45. The question resembles 2 Samuel 24:21. (IV, V)

[44] Elizabeth seemed to interpret the babe's movement as a sign of the things of which she spoke. She said **the babe leaped for joy**, indicating her understanding of the event (cf. notes at 1:14).

[45] The brief speech concluded with praise for Mary's faith (see Heb. 11:11), made sharper by contrast with

LUKE 1:46-48 *Magnificat*

⁴⁶And Mary said,
"My soul magnifies the Lord,
⁴⁷and my spirit rejoices in God my Savior,
⁴⁸for he has regarded the low estate of his handmaiden.
For, behold, henceforth all generations will call me blessed;

Zechariah. The change to the third person indicates verse 45 was a more formal prayer or blessing. **Blessed** is from a different Greek word (*makarios*) than in verse 42. The term, though frequent elsewhere, is found in Luke at 6:20, 21, 22; 7:23; 10:23; 11:27, 28; 12:37, 38, 43; 14:14, 15; 23:29. (VII)

[46] This poem, more like a meditation than a prayer or an address to Elizabeth, is called the *Magnificat*, after the first word of the Latin text. It is quite like Hannah's song in 1 Samuel 2:1-10. Both speeches show how God helps the poor and humble rather than the rich and powerful (see also Zeph. 2:3; Matt. 5:3) and how God has favored Israel since the promises to Abraham (see Deut. 7:6). Mary's praise to God was intensified beyond any normal reasons for doing so by her recognition of what he was doing through her.

[47] Rejoice is found elsewhere in Luke 10:21, but see the remarks on the cognate "gladness" at 1:14. Here the concept of salvation, not stressed previously in the book, is presented (see also 1 Sam. 2:1; Hab. 3:18; and on the expression **God my Savior** see 1 Tim. 2:3; Titus 2:13; Jude 25). The rest of the poem makes the idea more explicit.

[48] Mary's language is reminiscent of 1 Samuel 1:11 and 2:5. The verse indicates something of her humble circumstances and her self-effacement as she thankfully recognized the place God had given her (see Gen. 30:13; Luke 1:42; 11:27). This text, though showing the importance of Mary in God's scheme, certainly does not encourage worshiping her or granting any of the exorbitant claims made for her by some. Indeed, her attitude toward herself contrasts with that often accorded her in subsequent years.

God's Acts   LUKE 1:49-52

⁴⁹ for he who is mighty has done great things for me,
and holy is his name.
⁵⁰ And his mercy is on those who fear him from
generation to generation.
⁵¹ He has shown strength with his arm,
he has scattered the proud in the imagination of their hearts,
⁵² he has put down the mighty from their thrones,
and exalted those of low degree;

---

[49] See 1 Samuel 2:2; Psalm 111:9; 113:5; and the comments at 1:35. (VII)

[50] At this point Mary's song moves from herself to more universal concepts (see Ps. 103:13, 17).

[51] This verse begins a series of statements expressed by the Greek aorist tense (point action in the past). They may refer to God's past accomplishments or to his future deeds, spoken of in this way to indicate how sure they were of fulfillment, or to the actions which always characterize God. The **arm** of God was a symbol often used for his power (Ps. 89:10f.). On the scattering of **the proud**, see 1 Samuel 2:3; Psalm 138:6. This word for **proud** is always used in a bad sense in the New Testament.

Perhaps the classes specified in these and the following verses were indicated because such groups would have special significance to Luke's readers, or it may be that the expressions were used because of their familiarity from the Old Testament background. The themes of pride, humility, riches, and poverty are frequently presented in the gospel.

[52] On the demotion of **the mighty** and exaltation of the lowly, see 1 Samuel 2:4, 7; Job 5:11; 12:19; and Psalm 147:6. God would not oppose men just because they had positions of might, so the meaning must refer to those using might for wicked purposes. Is this indication of social revolution to be taken literally or figuratively? In the Old Testament depiction of God and the nations (Isa. 13-23; Jer. 46-51; Ezek. 25-32; Amos 1, 2), as well as in the ultimate outcome of history, it would be literal; but in the history of the time

LUKE 1:53-55 — God's Mercy

⁵³ he has filled the hungry with good things,
and the rich he has sent empty away.
⁵⁴ He has helped his servant Israel,
in remembrance of his mercy,
⁵⁵ as he spoke to our fathers,
to Abraham and to his posterity for ever."

---

of Jesus and the church, the spiritual sense is better, since Christianity is neither a political entity nor a theocracy. **Those of low degree** may have been the oppressed poor, as opposed to tyrannical rulers; or, in the Old Testament, they may have been Israel.

[53] Luke refers to **the hungry** also in 4:2; 6:3; and see especially 6:21, 25. Notice also 1 Samuel 2:5; Psalm 34:10; and Psalm 107:9. This passage is highly reminiscent of the appeal for social justice seen in certain Old Testament prophets, such as Amos. **Good things** is probably symbolic of the spiritual blessings of the new age.

The rich were probably oppressors, since in the Old Testament wealth was often looked upon as a token of God's blessings (Deut. 28) and normally would be seen that way unless the wickedness of such people were also known (but cf. Ps. 73, where the writer could not understand why the wicked should prosper). The verb form, be **rich,** is found here and at 12:21 in Luke. Note also 6:24.

[54] Here is summed up the history of God's acts for the people, with the circumstances of the song implying that the greatest act of all was imminent. God was helping, is helping, and will help! On **Israel** as God's **servant** see Isaiah 41:8f.

[55] The mercy of God in helping Israel is further explicated by connecting it with the Abrahamic promise (see Gen. 12:3; 13:14-17; 15:5; and cf. Micah 7:20; Luke 1:73). Luke mentions **Abraham** in 1:73; 3:8, 34; 13:16, 28; 16:22-25, 29, 30; 19:9; 20:37. The promise was **for ever,** which means, literally, unto the age.

The song has now progressed from Mary, to the general

Circumcision   LUKE 1:56-61

⁵⁶ And Mary remained with her about three months, and returned to her home.

⁵⁷ Now the time came for Elizabeth to be delivered, and she gave birth to a son. ⁵⁸ And her neighbors and kinsfolk heard that the Lord had shown great mercy to her, and they rejoiced with her. ⁵⁹ And on the eighth day they came to circumcise the child; and they would have named him Zechariah after his father, ⁶⁰ but his mother said, "Not so; he shall be called John." ⁶¹ And they said to her, "None of your kindred is called by this name."

---

goodness of God, to Israel. It has noted moral, social, and economic revolutions. There has been no direct word about Mary's son, but his work has been implied throughout. (V, VII)

[56] **Mary** probably stayed till John was born, though that birth is not mentioned till the next paragraph, since Luke has a way of rounding off one incident before going on to another (1:64, 67; 3:19f.; 8:37f.).

The Birth of the Baptist, 1:57-80

[57, 58] The popular reaction reintroduces the ideas of joy (1:14; see 15:6, 9; Rom. 12:15) and mercy (1:50). It is possible that Elizabeth's situation might not have been generally known, since she had been in seclusion. There is no indication the neighbors knew of the supernatural nature of the conception and birth.

[59] Genesis 17:10-14 records the institution of circumcision, and Leviticus 12:3 specified **the eighth day** (cf. Phil. 3:5). There is no record in the Old Testament of a name being given on **the eighth day,** but it was apparently the custom in Palestine in Zechariah's time. Abram's name was changed at his circumcision, but this does not seem to have become a custom in the Old Testament period. In the Hellenistic world a child was named seven to ten days after birth, and the Jews might have adopted such a form and connected it with circumcision.

[60, 61] It was assumed the child would bear the paternal

LUKE 1:62-65 — *Named John*

⁶²And they made signs to his father, inquiring what he would have him called. ⁶³And he asked for a writing tablet, and wrote, "His name is John." And they all marveled. ⁶⁴And immediately his mouth was opened and his tongue loosed, and he spoke, blessing God. ⁶⁵And fear came on all their neighbors. And all these things were talked about through all the hill country of Judea;

---

name according to Jewish custom, especially an only child of old age. Yet Elizabeth insisted he **be called John**. Indeed, the entire episode is built around the point. Elizabeth apparently shared her husband's faith regarding the angelic giving of the name.

[62] The people might have thought Elizabeth was acting simply on her own initiative, or that Zechariah had been unable to communicate his wishes adequately, or that the two disagreed. The **signs** implied he was deaf as well as dumb.

[63] The wooden **tablet** either would be covered with parchment or have a hollow into which a film of wax was poured. His answer was given firmly, so there was no doubt. Thus an act of faith counteracted his previous failure. In the whole series of events Luke is asking whether men will believe God's promises. And because Zechariah came to believe, his speech returned. The witnesses **marveled** that he agreed in upsetting the expected adherence to tradition.

[64] With the fulfillment of those things mentioned in 1:13, speech was restored to the father. The further predictions of Gabriel's poem awaited later fulfillment. **Immediately** is found ten times in Luke, six times in Acts, and only twice in the rest of the New Testament.

Zechariah's **blessing** (see notes at 1:12) may have been the subsequent speech, or some other expostulation. (VII)

[65] On **fear**, see the notes at 1:12. **Talked about** is used in the New Testament only here and Luke 6:11. This statement, and the next verse, may indicate something of Luke's sources. Some of these people may have followed John the Baptist and Jesus, and later become Christians, so that Luke

Benedictus LUKE 1:66-68

⁶⁶and all who heard them laid them up in their hearts, saying, "What then will this child be?" For the hand of the Lord was with him.

⁶⁷And his father Zechariah was filled with the Holy Spirit, and prophesied, saying,

⁶⁸"Blessed be the Lord God of Israel,
for he has visited and redeemed his people,

---

learned from them. The fact that the stories were spread would also help give Theophilus surer knowledge (1:1, 4).

[66] Knowledge of any or all of the events from Gabriel's appearance to John's circumcision would increase amazement about the child. It seems logical, in view of his returned speech and the need to explain the boy's name, that Zechariah would tell his experiences. Also, the lad's subsequent life was unusual.

Often **the hand of the Lord** refers to God's power (cf. the power of men in Luke 9:44; and the hand of God in Acts 4:28, 30; 11:21; 13:11). This is related to the Holy Spirit in Luke 1:15. It could involve God's protection (cf. Jer. 26:24), as well as the work and power given him by the Lord. As in the previous paragraph, Luke closes out this episode before moving to something new.

[67] **Zechariah** is identified as **his father**, perhaps indicating the focus of attention now moves to John. In addition to speech, **the Spirit** (see notes at 1:5) granted **Zechariah** special insights. He elaborates the closing ideas of the *Magnificat*. This speech is called the *Benedictus*, after the first word of the Latin.

[68] In verses 68-75 Zechariah stresses God's fulfillment of the promises through the prophets and of the oath sworn to Abraham. The Davidic line is to be continued. The speech specifies the nature of the blessings attendant upon the fulfillment with such words as **visited, redeemed,** "salvation," "perform mercy promised," "remember covenant," "deliverance," and "serve." The section is a magnificent delineation of the benefits of the end time being ushered

LUKE 1:68-71 *Salvation*

⁶⁹ and has raised up a horn of salvation for us
in the house of his servant David,
⁷⁰ as he spoke by the mouth of his holy prophets from of old,
⁷¹ that we should be saved from our enemies,
and from the hand of all who hate us;

---

in by John. Verses 76-79 continue the theme by specifying the unique role John would play in these events. Note the eschatological terms "salvation," "forgiveness," "mercy," "give light," and "guide into peace." The speech is a miniature compendium of theology regarding the blessings of the last time.

On the blessing of **God**, see Psalms 41:13f.; 72:18; 89:52; and 106:48. God's visitation often refers in the Old Testament to his special incursions into history to make known his will either in mercy or in judgment. The Hebrew term is frequently translated in the Septuagint by the Greek term Luke uses here. Luke adds a new feature to the idea in associating it with redemption and salvation, so that its import becomes messianic. Luke is the only New Testament writer to use the Greek term in the sense of God's action (1:78; 7:16; Acts 15:14; cf. Heb. 2:6, which quotes Ps. 8:4; see also Luke 19:44).

The concept of redemption was not specifically noted in the *Magnificat*. The term is found in the New Testament only here; 2:38; and Hebrews 9:12. As with many elements of the present poem, any apparent political significance (drawn from the traditional messianic language) the words may seem to have is transcended by the deeper spiritual fulfillment wrought in Christ. For Luke and his readers words like "redemption," **people**, "enemy," and "covenant" would have a transformed Christian meaning, though Jewish hopes of the time of Zechariah may have viewed them nationalistically. (II)

[69-71] The **salvation** concept of verse 69 is elaborated in verse 71 (see Pss. 18:17; 106:10). On **all who hate us** compare 6:22; 19:14; and 21:17. (II, VII)

Covenant Promises   **LUKE 1:72-76**

⁷²to perform the mercy promised to our fathers,
and to remember his holy covenant,
⁷³the oath which he swore to our father Abraham, ⁷⁴to grant us that we, being delivered from the hand of our enemies, might serve him without fear,
⁷⁵in holiness and righteousness before him all the days of our life.
⁷⁶And you, child, will be called the prophet of the Most High; for you will go before the Lord to prepare his ways.

---

[72] Here the purpose of the idea begun in verse 69 is expressed (see Pss. 105:8, 42; 106:45; Micah 7:20). In this and the following verse God is said to fulfill his **mercy, covenant,** and "oath" (see Lev. 26:42; Acts 3:25).

[73] The poem has progressed from prophets to fathers, to Sinai, to **Abraham,** with each step going farther back in the fulfillment scheme (see Gen. 17:7; 22:16-18; 26:3f.; Ex. 2:24; Jer. 11:5; Luke 1:55). Verses 77-79 indicate the present verses are to be taken in the spiritual sense. Rather than quoting the direct promise to **Abraham,** the text explicates consequences of the Abrahamic promise.

[74] The deliverance from **enemies** restates the idea of verse 71, with a result of the deliverance added (see Jer. 30:8,9). There is no note of vengeance on the **enemies,** but only the idea of freedom from them (cf. 6:27, 35), in contrast with the frequent Old Testament curses upon the writer's foes (cf. Pss. 58:6-11; 137:7-9). (I, II)

[76] Here the *Benedictus* moves to specific prediction concerning John. Jesus was the "Son of the Most High" (note verse 32), and John would be **the prophet of the Most High.** Prophecy had ceased to appear in Israel (see 1 Macc. 4:46; 9:27; 14:41), but John would break this silence (1:16f. had already implied this). In a sense Zechariah had already broken the silence (vs. 67; cf. Anna, 2:36). Yet John was also more than a prophet (Luke 7:26). His task was to involve heralding the Lord (see Mal. 3:1; 4:5; Isa. 40:3). He would

LUKE 1:77-79 *Forgiveness*

⁷⁷ to give knowledge of salvation to his people
in the forgiveness of their sins,
⁷⁸ through the tender mercy of our God,
when the day shall dawn upon ʲ us from on high
⁷⁹ to give light to those who sit in darkness and in the
shadow of death,
to guide our feet into the way of peace."

ʲ Or *whereby the dayspring will visit*. Other ancient authorities read *since the dayspring has visited*.

---

be like one going through the countryside announcing and making all necessary preparations for the coming of a sovereign. In this case, it was to prepare people for what God would do through Christ, as explained in verses 77-79.

[77] This would involve **forgiveness of sins** — a dimension which the concept of **salvation** had not been given previously in Luke (cf. 3:3; Mark 1:4). John's baptism for **forgiveness** was a sign of the messianic age. And the performance of his task forced the Jews to see themselves — and not just the Gentiles — as sinners in need of divine **forgiveness**. The word for **forgiveness** is found five times in the gospel. Three cases refer to remission of **sins** (here; 3:3; 24:47). In the other two cases (4:18) it is translated "release" and "set at liberty." These were messianic signs (from Isa. 61:1). Thus the claim to bring **forgiveness** was an indication of Jesus' Christhood (see 4:17-26). In Acts the term is found five times (2:38; 5:31; 10:43; 13:38; 26:18) and all refer to **forgiveness of sins**. Thus the expression **forgiveness of sins** is eight times in the Lukan writings, and the word for **forgiveness** is only found seven times in the rest of the New Testament. See Jeremiah 31:31-34.

The word for **sins** is in Luke at 3:3; 5:20, 21, 23, 24; 7:47, 48, 49; 11:4; and 24:47, and is always in a context where **forgiveness** is offered.

[78] The word for **tender** originally meant the "inward parts" and later came to refer to the seat of the emotions, with the word "heart" the nearest equivalent.

[79] The figure here is of travelers sitting terrified in

John's Youth LUKE 1:79—2:1

⁸⁰ And the child grew and became strong in spirit, and he was in the wilderness till the day of his manifestation to Israel.

¹ In those days a decree went out from Caesar Augustus that all the world should be enrolled.

---

fear of darkness, when they would be at the mercy of enemies or ravaging animals (see Ps. 107:10-14). The idea of **light** is reminiscent of Malachi 4:2 and Isaiah 9:2 (cf. also Isa. 42:7f.; Matt. 4:16; and 2 Peter 1:19). The expression testified to the depths of humanity's need.

Luke lays great stress on the concept of **peace**, using the word in the gospel at 2:14, 29; 7:50; 8:48; 10:5, 6; 11:21; 12:51; 14:32; 19:38, 42, as well as seven times in Acts. The other gospels use the word only a combined total of nine times (cf. also Isa. 59:8; Rom. 3:17). (II, V, VII)

[80] About thirty years are comprehended in this verse. Like Moses, John went to **the wilderness** (cf. also Judges 13:24f.). He might be seen as preparing **Israel** for a new "exodus." The text does not specify the age at which he began such a life, nor why he went, nor what his parents thought of it. He probably lived in the desolate area on the west-northwest side of the Dead Sea, though some argue **wilderness** simply means away from towns and villages. The day of his **manifestation** was probably when God sent him from there preaching (see Matt. 3:1; cf. Luke 3:23).

In the light of the Dead Sea Scrolls and what little is known of the Essenes, many theories have been suggested regarding the relation of John to these peoples. He may have lived in the same area, and there is some similarity in their teachings. However, there are also marked differences. It is likely that John knew of and was in contact with such groups, but John must be seen as a man of God to himself and not simply categorized as one of a religious community.

The Birth of Jesus, 2:1-20 (Matt. 1:18—2:23)

[1] In his appeal to the Gentile mind, Luke connected

LUKE 2:1, 2 — Enrollment

²**This was the first enrollment, when Quirinius was governor of Syria.**

---

the Lord's birth with the reign of **Caesar Augustus** (27 B.C.-A.D. 14) and the background of Roman history. His **decree** (lit., "dogma," meaning here "public decree, ordinance," see Acts 16:4; 17:7; Eph. 2:15; Col. 2:14) was for the entire Roman empire (**all the world**). This enrollment, not mentioned outside the Bible, may have been a registration for taxation purposes and may have continued for some time. Possibly it dealt with information concerning names, families, professions, and wealth, as well as being an assessment of taxes.

Though it is impossible to establish the date of Jesus' birth with certainty, it probably occurred near 6 B.C. Verses 1 and 2 have aroused some question; first, because this enrollment is not mentioned outside the Bible; and second, with regard to the governorship of Quirinius (discussed with verse 2). The former problem, though not completely solved, has been treated in such a way as to vindicate Luke's accuracy as a historian. The confused state of records from the period, coupled with the precarious nature of arguments from silence, disallow any solid grounds for doubting Luke. Historical research reveals that **Augustus** held a census of Roman citizens in 8 B.C. and another in A.D. 6. The first of these may have been delayed in its administration in Palestine till near the time of Jesus' birth.

[2] It is known that **Quirinius was governor of Syria** in A.D. 6, 7. It is also known that the governors of Syria from 9 B.C. till 4 B.C. were, in turn, Saturninus and Varus. This leaves no room for **Quirinius** at the time described in the text. However, a damaged inscription, now in the Lateran Museum and thought to refer to **Quirinius**, indicates he served two terms. Ramsay argues his first term would have been 10 B.C., before Saturninus. This, however, still does not solve the problem. Some suggest that the census may have begun during his first governorship but was delayed

³ And all went to be enrolled, each to his own city. ⁴ And Joseph also went up from Galilee, from the city of Nazareth, to Judea, to the city of David, which is called Bethlehem, because he was of the house and lineage of David, ⁵ to be enrolled with Mary, his betrothed, who was with child. ⁶ And while they were there, the time came for her to be delivered.

in its execution in Palestine. This appears to be forced, especially in view of the evidence above (verse 1) that the census of Augustus began in 8 B.C. Others note that the word translated **governor** was a general term and might refer to any office of rulership. Thus **Quirinius** may have had another office when Jesus was born, with special concern for **the enrollment**. Sir William Ramsay has noted that other occasions can be documented when two men with the title of "legatus Caesaris" were appointed to one province because one of them was expected to be fully occupied with command of the army. Such might have been the case here.

Though none of these suggestions is completely satisfactory, certain things need to be remembered. First, the events described in the text can at least be shown to be possible. Second, not all of the evidence is now available, so conclusions must be tentative. Also, indications of Luke's careful research and historical veracity elsewhere speak for his reliability on this point. Luke's knowledge of the censuses is shown by Acts 5:37, and he indicates the census here was before that in Acts (which was A.D. 6).

[3, 4] It was apparently a Jewish custom to go to the ancestral home, though not all the details of this procedure are known. When **Joseph went** the eighty miles to **Bethlehem**, apparently the events of Matthew 1:18-25 had already occurred. **Bethlehem** was called **the city of David** because David's father had lived there (1 Sam. 17:12ff., 58). **Joseph** was one of David's descendants (1:27). The greatest Davidic king would be born in **the city of** the first **David**.

[5, 6] **Mary** was not obliged to make the trip for

LUKE 2:6, 7 *Jesus' Birth*

⁷And she gave birth to her first-born son and wrapped him in swaddling cloths, and laid him in a manger, because there was no place for them in the inn.

---

enrollment purposes, and it was doubtless a strain for her. But she and Joseph would likely not want to be separated when the child's birth was near. Whether the world saw them as still **betrothed** or as married, they had not to this time consummated their relationship (see Matt. 1:25).

The text does not specify how long they stayed in Bethlehem. They may not have wished to risk a return trip even after performing the requirements of the enrollment. Some think they deliberately remained to fulfill Micah 5:2, concerning the Messiah's birthplace.

[7] How simply so profound an event is narrated! The circumstances of the **birth** formed a striking contrast to the child's real nature. Luke shows how ordinary were the events in which God acted extraordinarily. Reference to Mary's **first-born** is not conclusive evidence for the birth of later children to her. **Swaddling cloths** were customarily used to clothe new-born children. A square of cloth had a longer strip of cloth attached at one corner, and this was wrapped around the child after the square was put in place.

A **manger** or feeding trough became the child's crib. Thus an infant in an animal feeder became the central point of world history. Joseph was reduced to staying in a stable because **the inn** was full. Yet the accommodations, though low by modern standards, may not have been so dismal as sometimes thought, especially considering the less than satisfactory quarters at inns in those days. The text does not say why **the inn** was so crowded. Perhaps it was because of the number of people present for the enrollment. Others suggest there may have been a feast in Jerusalem, and inns as far as Bethlehem were filled with pilgrims.

This paragraph of the Bible has begun with Caesar and ended with Jesus. The world of that day would have regarded

Shepherds LUKE 2:8-11

⁸And in that region there were shepherds out in the field, keeping watch over their flock by night. ⁹And an angel of the Lord appeared to them, and the glory of the Lord shone round them, and they were filled with fear. ¹⁰And the angel said to them, "Be not afraid; for behold, I bring you good news of a great joy which will come to all the people; ¹¹for to you is born this day in the city of David a Savior, who is Christ the Lord.

---

the former as much the more important, but the God of history has reversed that judgment.

[8] The announcement to the **shepherds** continues the theme of the "commonness" of the circumstances surrounding the event. One would scarcely have expected such people to be the first to hear the news, yet they may have yearned more for Messiah's advent than the religiously elite of the land (cf. Micah 4:8). It has been suggested that these **shepherds** may have kept the temple flocks. While popularly the appearance is pictured in December, it is impossible to ascertain the exact time of year.

[9] Again there was an angelic appearance (see 1:11-20, 26-38), with the additional mention in this case of divine **glory** (a word found in 2:9, 14, 32; 4:6; 9:26, 31, 32; 12:27; 14:10; 17:18; 19:38; 21:27; 24:26).

[10] On **be not afraid** see 1:12. In the words of the messenger two favorite themes of Luke, **joy** (see notes on 1:14, 58) and universalism, appear again. On **bring good news,** see notes at 1:19.

[11] The announcement had tremendous significance, for it was what the people had longingly awaited. In it are the three great Christian claims made about Jesus. He is **Savior, Christ,** and **Lord.** On Jesus as **Savior** see 1:47, 69, 71, 77, and compare Matthew 1:21. The concept would have both political and religious meaning to the Jews. **Christ** indicated the one anointed to be king. The term is also found in Luke 2:26; 3:15; 4:41; 9:20; 20:41; 22:67; 23:2, 35, 39; 24:26, 46. **Lord** was the Old Testament title for God. (I, II, IV)

LUKE 2:12-16 *Peace*

¹² And this will be a sign for you: you will find a babe wrapped in swaddling cloths and lying in a manger." ¹³ And suddenly there was with the angel a multitude of the heavenly host praising God and saying,

¹⁴ "Glory to God in the highest,
  and on earth peace among men with whom he is pleased!"ᵍ

¹⁵ When the angels went away from them into heaven, the shepherds said to one another, "Let us go over to Bethlehem and see this thing that has happened, which the Lord has made known to us."

  ᵍ Other ancient authorities read, *peace, good will among men*

---

[12] As to Zechariah and Mary, so **a sign** was given to the shepherds. This vindicated the truthfulness of the announcement, as well as helped them find the child. The **swaddling cloths** would be normal, but the **manger** would not, so this was the chief element of the sign. (VII)

[13] Upon the angel's announcement, heaven burst into praise (on angels and angelic ministry cf. Matt. 18:10; Luke 16:22; Acts 5:19; 12:7ff., 15; Heb. 1:14; 1 Peter 1:12; see also notes at 1:11). Praise is a favorite verb with Luke (see notes on 2:20). The word used here is found seven times in the Lukan writings and only twice in the rest of the New Testament. The impression on the shepherds would be intensified by the song of the heavenly choir. (V)

[14] This hymn is called the *Gloria in Excelsis* from the Latin text (see 1:46, 68). In addition to the prior angelic words, here **peace** was an intrinsic part of the news. The word means that entire harmony of life which is found, perfectly, only in God. See notes at 1:79, and compare also Isaiah 52:7; 57:19; Acts 10:36; Ephesians 2:17 and 6:15. There are variant renderings of the expression here translated **among men with whom he is well pleased,** but the text translated by the RSV, which is probably best, indicates the idea of the favor with which God regards his elect.

[15, 16] Their hasty trip indicates their eagerness to confirm the message. It must have involved effort and

Praise LUKE 2:15-20

[16] And they went with haste, and found **Mary and Joseph, and the babe lying in a manger.** [17] And when they saw it they made known the saying which had been told them concerning the child; [18] and all who heard it **wondered at what the** shepherds told them. [19] But Mary kept all these things, pondering them in her heart. [20] And the shepherds returned, glorifying and praising God for all they had heard and seen, as it had been told them.

---

inconvenience (e.g., arranging for the sheep) to go. The Greek word for **found** indicates some intensity, perhaps even difficulty, in the search. But ultimately they discovered the place. They must have been struck by the contrast between the splendor of the announcement and the commonness of the babe's situation. And aside from the fulfillment of the angelic word, there was no indication from anything else they saw to confirm their messianic hopes. (V)

[17, 18] It was only an infant, and thus the kingdom could not come at that moment. Nonetheless, the word was spread about the visit of the angel, and perhaps the hearers included Simeon and Anna (2:25-38). Yet people **wondered at** the news. Such stories, as preserved, would be recalled and invested with fuller meaning as the church came to engage in further reflection about its Lord.

[19] The text says expressly that **Mary** remembered (see also 2:51). She, as well as others, may have been Luke's source of information. She pondered (the word is peculiar to Luke), and it may have been her continued reflections which made her recall so well that she was able to give Luke such a wealth of intimate detail.

[20] **The shepherds returned,** different men than they were before. Note how Luke dwells on the idea of praise (1:25, 38, 46-55, 64, 68-79; 2:13f., 28; 5:25f.; 7:16; 13:13; 17:15, 18; 18:43; 19:37; 23:47; 24:53; Acts 2:47). The verb for **glorifying** is used in Luke 2:20; 4:15; 5:25, 26; 7:16; 13:13; 17:15; 18:43; and 23:47. In every case but one (referring to Christ) the reference is to glorifying **God.** Such

LUKE 2:21, 22 *Named Jesus*

²¹ And at the end of eight days, when he was circumcised, he was called Jesus, the name given by the angel before he was conceived in the womb.

²² And when the time came for their purification according to the law of Moses, they brought him up to Jerusalem to present him to the Lord

---

circumstances would not be forgotten, but theirs was the task of patient waiting till the full fruition of God's promises should appear. (V)

The Circumcision of Jesus and the Presentation in the Temple, 2:21-40

The obedience of the central figures to the law of the Lord is especially prominent in the rest of the chapter. The word "law" is used here five times, more than in all the rest of the gospel (2:22, 23, 24, 27, 39; also 10:26; 16:16, 17; 24:44).

[21] **Jesus**, "born under the law" (Gal. 4:4) **was circumcised** as the law demanded (see notes on 1:59). This circumcision differs from that of John (1:59-63), in the absence of friends and relatives. Here, as there, the meaning of **the name** (see 1:31), rather than the circumcision, bears central significance (see Matt. 1:21, where the significance of **the name** is made more explicit). (VII)

[22] In verses 22-24 and 27 two things are intertwined in such a way that the record is at times unclear. They are the mother's **purification** and the child's presentation. **Purification,** described in Leviticus 12, was to cleanse the mother from the ritual uncleanness due to childbirth. This was not because sex or procreation was evil but because a bodily issue rendered her unclean (see Lev. 15:16-30). The presentation was probably the redemption of the first-born son (Ex. 13:2, 12; 22:29; 34:19; Num. 3:12; 18:15f.). Numbers 18:15f. specified that the appropriate offering was five shekels of silver, to be paid when the child was a month old. Apparently custom allowed some latitude if the deed were done near the specified time. Here it would be forty

Purification LUKE 2:22-24

²³ **(as it is written in the law of the Lord, "Every male that opens the womb shall be called holy to the Lord") ²⁴ and to offer a sacrifice according to what is said in the law of the Lord, "a pair of turtledoves, or two young pigeons."**

---

days, since that was the time the woman had to wait for her **purification** after a son's birth.

Luke uses *katharismos* for **purification,** avoiding the term *katharsis,* which meant menstruation and which might lead Gentile readers to misunderstand the nature of the situation. There is a problem in noting that it was the time of **their purification,** since neither father nor child were normally considered unclean after childbirth. Perhaps the term was general because indirectly the whole family was involved; or it may have been meant to include both presentation and **purification.**

The trip **to Jerusalem** was a short one, doubtless before the visit of the Magi (Matt. 2:1-12), since they would scarcely go **to Jerusalem** after Herod's slaughter of the innocents. Also, the fact that Herod killed children two years and under indicated Jesus may have been about that age when the murders took place.

This is the first time the gospel mentions **Jerusalem** by name. Other references to the city by name are 2:25, 38, 41, 43, 45; 4:9; 5:17; 6:17; 9:31, 51, 53; 10:30; 13:4, 22, 33, 34; 17:11; 18:31; 19:11, 28; 21:20, 24; 23:7, 28; 24:13, 18, 33, 47, 49, 52. This Greek form is found once in Matthew, not at all in Mark and John, and only eleven times in the rest of the New Testament, excluding Acts (where there are thirty-five references). The **Jerusalem** theme is very important in Luke's framework. This will become increasingly clear later in the gospel, especially in the last journey to the city (beginning 9:51). See the discussion in the introduction, page 17. Other references to **Moses** in the gospel are at 5:14; 9:30, 33; 16:29, 31; 20:28, 37; 24:27, 44.

[23, 24] Verse 23 is similar to the Old Testament references cited in the comments on verse 22 concerning the

LUKE 2:25, 26 — *Simeon*

[25] Now there was a man in Jerusalem, whose name was Simeon, and this man was righteous and devout, looking for the consolation of Israel, and the Holy Spirit was upon him. [26] And it had been revealed to him by the Holy Spirit that he should not see death before he had seen the Lord's Christ.

---

redemption of the firstborn. Verse 24 describes the **sacrifice** for purification offered by those who could not afford the costlier gift of a lamb (Lev. 12:6-8). The sacrificial animals were sold in the temple precincts (Matt. 21:12). It is not clear why Luke intertwines these two rituals in the telling of the story. The two were simultaneous, apparently, and perhaps it was not necessary for Luke's Gentile readers to make a precise distinction. (VIII)

[25] Nothing is known of **Simeon** aside from what the present context reveals. Preeminent in his and Anna's (vss. 36-38) character was their piety. They may represent such **devout** Israelites as longed anxiously for the Messiah and were prepared to accept him. **Devout** is unique to Luke in the New Testament (Acts 2:5; 8:2; 22:12). His recognition of the child's significance shows in microcosm that pious Hebrews would find the God-ordained completion of their faith in Jesus (see Acts 24:14f.; 26:7f.). **The consolation** for which Simeon looked might reflect traditions which described the messianic age as a time of comfort for the troubled (see Isa. 40:1; 49:13; 52:9; and cf. Gen. 49:18; Ps. 119:166; Luke 1:68; 6:24; and 23:51).

Note also in verses 25-27 further references to **the Holy Spirit** (see notes on 1:15). Perhaps it was only at Jesus' visit, or shortly before, that these revelations to **Simeon** had come. On **righteous** see 1:6.

[26] Apparently Simeon was old and longed for **death** (see 9:27; and cf. John 8:51; Heb. 11:5). The revelation about **the Lord's Christ** may have been unclear to him until the insight that came when he saw the child. In this he would recognize the dawning of the messianic age. This passage prepares for further messianic signs to be depicted

Nunc Dimittis LUKE 2:27-32

²⁷And inspired by the Spirit* he came into the temple; and when the parents brought in the child Jesus, to do for him according to the custom of the law, ²⁸he took him up in his arms and blessed God and said,
²⁹"Lord, now lettest thou thy servant depart in peace,
according to thy word;
³⁰for mine eyes have seen thy salvation
³¹which thou hast prepared in the presence of all peoples,
³²a light for revelation to the Gentiles,
and for glory to thy people Israel."

* Or *in the Spirit*

---

in the gospel. Simeon represented those in Israel whose ardent hopes for the Messiah were at the point of realization (on **Christ**, see 2:11). (IV, V, VII)

[27, 28] This probably refers to the presentation part of the ritual. The context implies that God led Simeon **into the temple** at this time and for this purpose. Thus a saint in Israel blessed the bringer of new Israel, and then awaited the longed-for death. On **blessed**, see 1:42.

The temple, in Luke's presentation, plays an important role at the beginning, and the end, of Jesus' life and in the beginning of the life of the Christian community (cf. Acts 2).

[29] This prayer, called *Nunc Dimittis* from the Latin, uses the language that a slave might use in asking to be freed. The word for **Lord** (*despota*) implies the idea of an absolute ruler, like a slave master. Simeon, his long watch over, longed for release as a slave might yearn for freedom, not even caring to await the coming kingdom (cf. Gen. 15:15; 46:30). On **peace**, see 1:69.

[30] Simeon did not speak of the child specifically but of his significance. The **salvation** itself, not yet fact, had been accomplished in prospect in the infant (cf. Isa. 40:5; 52:10; Luke 3:6). The word for **salvation** used here is elsewhere in 2:36; Acts 28:28, and only one other place in the New Testament. (II)

[31, 32] The very point for which this story was included

LUKE 2:32-35 — *Fall and Rising*

³³And his father and his mother marveled at what was said about him; ³⁴and Simeon blessed them and said to Mary his mother,

"Behold, this child is set for the fall and rising of many in Israel,
and for a sign that is spoken against
³⁵(and a sword will pierce through your own soul also),
that thoughts out of many hearts may be revealed."

³⁶And there was a prophetess, Anna, the daughter of Phanuel, of the tribe of Asher; she was of a great age, having lived with her husband seven years from her virginity, ³⁷and as

---

may well have been its universalistic thrust. Here, as can be seen from the comparison of Isaiah 42:6 and 49:6, the child is seen as fulfilling the servant mission of Israel. (I, V, VII)

[33] The suddenness and unexpectedness of the event, and the nature of the announcement (though its content was not new to them) likely contributed to the amazement of the parents.

[34] Verses 34f. deal with **Mary**, again indicating that she may have been Luke's source. These are somber words, in contrast to the joy of the angel's revelation. **Fall and rising** probably show the differing reactions to Christ, and their consequences. Compare the idea of the stone which was a stone of stumbling and a corner stone (Isa. 8:14; Rom. 9:33; Eph. 2:20; 1 Peter 2:7f; as well as Luke 1:51-53). On Jesus as the **sign spoken against** see Mark 6:3; Luke 4:28; Acts 28:22; 1 Corinthians 1:23; 2 Corinthians 2:16; and Hebrews 12:3. On **blessed,** see 1:42.

[35] The figure of the **sword** described the grief her son's suffering would cause Mary (see John 19:25). In his work, which would be opposed, Jesus would stand as the great barer of secrets. Men's reactions to him would reveal their true natures. See the section on Jesus knowing hearts in the introduction (III, IV, V). On reactions to and rejection of Jesus, see introduction. (VI, VII)

Anna

a widow till she was eighty-four. She did not depart from the temple, worshiping with fasting and prayer night and day. ³⁸ And coming up at that very hour she gave thanks to God, and spoke of him to all who were looking for the redemption of Jerusalem.

³⁹ And when they had performed everything according to the law of the Lord, they returned into Galilee, to their own city, Nazareth. ⁴⁰ And the child grew, and became strong, filled with wisdom; and the favor of God was upon him.

[36, 37] The text does not explain the nature of Anna's prophesying (cf. Ex. 15:20; Judges 4:4) or how long she had been endowed with such powers. Perhaps the term primarily explains her speaking as she did at this time. **Anna** was a truly devout woman, of the sort Luke has been emphasizing in this chapter. She was constantly at **the temple** performing acts of piety (cf. 1 Tim. 5:5). Luke especially notes her prayers, as one might expect (see notes at 1:10, 13).

[38] Anna's words were no doubt triggered by the significance of the child and formed an "amen" to Simeon's speech. She may have had a prophetic foreknowledge of Jesus' messiahship. The concept of **redemption** (see 1:68; 24:21) stresses Luke's emphasis on **Jerusalem** as the center from which God would spread his salvation (see notes on 2:22). Apparently Anna continued in subsequent days to speak of these things, since all who looked for the **redemption of Jerusalem** were not there when she met the family of Joseph. (II)

[39] Again here **law**-keeping is emphasized. It would be at this point, chronologically, that the visit of the Magi and the flight into Egypt would occur (Matt. 2:1-23). The former, indicating a Gentile reaction to the Lord's birth, might seem the sort of thing Luke would tell if he knew of it.

[40] In Jesus the ideal of humanity is realized for the first time. This verse emphasizes his physical and mental growth, as verse 52 includes also the spiritual and social.

LUKE 2:41-44   *Jesus at Twelve*

⁴¹**Now his parents went to Jerusalem every year at the feast of the Passover.** ⁴²**And when he was twelve years old, they went up according to custom;** ⁴³**and when the feast was ended, as they were returning, the boy Jesus stayed behind in Jerusalem. His parents did not know it,** ⁴⁴**but supposing him to be in the company they went a day's journey, and they sought him among their kinsfolk and acquaintances;**

The next paragraph (verses 41-51) is a commentary on the boy's **wisdom** (a word found in Luke at 2:52; 7:35; 11:31, 49; 21:15).

Jesus at Twelve Years, 2:41-52

[41] This is the only event the gospels record from Jesus' boyhood. By this time there was no more fear that harm would come to the child in **Jerusalem** (see notes on 2:22). **The Passover** is described in Exodus 23:15 and Deuteronomy 16:1-8. According to Deuteronomy 16:16 Jewish men were required to attend the three great feasts (Unleavened Bread or **Passover,** Weeks or Pentecost, and Tabernacles or Booths) each year. But by the time of Jesus most Palestinian Jews simply tried to go **to Jerusalem** for one of the three each year, preferably **Passover.** The law did not require women to go, though some rabbinical teaching did, and Mary's going was a tribute to her dedication to the law.

[42] Some argue that at twelve a Jewish lad became a "son of the law," assuming an adult relationship to Jewish religious ordinances. Others maintain that this was not recognized till age thirteen. If the latter were true, possibly in the year preceding the father acquainted his son with the duties and requirements he would soon assume. At any rate, the point seems to be that when Jesus made an adult religious decision, or when an insight is given into his feelings, "he must be in his Father's house."

[43, 44] Why did Jesus stay **in Jerusalem?** Was his loss an accident? Perhaps. But verse 49 seems to indicate his

In the Temple — LUKE 2:43-50

⁴⁵ and when they did not find him, they returned to Jerusalem, seeking him. ⁴⁶ After three days they found him in the temple, sitting among the teachers, listening to them and asking them questions; ⁴⁷ and all who heard him were amazed at his understanding and his answers.

---

deliberate intent to stay. If so, it was a testimony that at this stage of his life he recognized an even higher responsibility than that to his parents (see 14:26). The **parents** were unaware of his absence. Since a large caravan of pilgrims would return to Galilee, it is likely they supposed that he was in some other part of the entourage and would join them that night when they stopped. Or if, as some suggest, the women went on ahead because of their slower rate of travel, both father and mother may have assumed the boy was with the other.

[45, 46] Though several explanations have been offered for the **three days,** it is logical to see the first as the day of travel from the city, the second as the day's travel back, and the third as the day on which Jesus was found. Where had he stayed during this time? Had those at the temple lodged and cared for him? Whatever the case, he was found in dialogue with **the teachers** (cf. Matt. 26:55). Members of the Sanhedrin offered religious instruction during the festivals and on sabbaths, and since the Feast of Unleavened Bread may still have been in progress (see Ex. 12:15, 18), that could have been the case here. Could any of the members of the Sanhedrin mentioned later in the New Testament have been at this gathering (Gamaliel, Nicodemus, Joseph of Arimathaea)?

Jesus respected those from whom he could learn. They, in turn, were amazed by his insight (verse 47), so unusual for a boy of twelve, especially one without rabbinic training. (IV)

[47-50] Jesus' first recorded words expressed a necessity to be where he was and said much about his feelings and

⁴⁸ And when they saw him they were astonished; and his mother said to him, "Son, why have you treated us so? Behold, your father and I have been looking for you anxiously." ⁴⁹ And he said to them, "How is it that you sought me? Did you not know that I must be in my Father's house?" ⁵⁰ And they did not understand the saying which he spoke to them. ⁵¹ And he went down with them and was obedient to them; and his mother kept all these things in her heart.

---

character (cf. 23:46). These words are no doubt the reason why the story is recorded. The superficial meaning of the statement may be to inquire why they didn't look for him in the temple right away, knowing his character and how he would love to be there (cf. Ps. 26:8; 27:4). But it was obvious to them that more was involved. Another translation could be "I must be at my Father's business," but the point would be the same. Interestingly, from this time onward neither Mary nor Jesus spoke of Joseph as his father. (VI, IX)

The contrast between **your Father** of verse 48 and **my** Father of verse 49 is striking. In this statement Jesus was expressing the transcendence of a higher relationship, made even more amazing in comparison with verse 52. But his parents had a great deal of puzzling to do yet about his words, as would others later (9:45; 18:34). This was in spite of what they already knew of him from the circumstances of his birth.

Certain elements of this first Passover seem to anticipate the last Passover of Jesus' life. There are questions in the temple, the absence of Jesus, his reappearance after three days, astonishment (here Mary, there the disciples), and a trip from Jerusalem. (V)

[51] Jesus left nothing to be desired as an ideal Jewish boy. His father is mentioned here for the last time. Had he died by the time of Jesus' personal ministry? On Mary's keeping of **these things,** see 1:29; 2:19. (IV)

John the Baptist   LUKE 2:52—3:1

⁵²And Jesus increased in wisdom and in stature¹, and in favor with God and man.

¹In the fifteenth year of the reign of Tiberius Caesar, Pontius Pilate being governor of Judea, and Herod being tetrarch of Galilee, and his brother Philip tetrarch of the region of Ituraea and Trachonitis, and Lysanias tetrarch of Abilene,

¹ Or *years*

---

[52] This verse summarizes the rest of Jesus' life till he was thirty (see 2:40). It may be based on 1 Samuel 2:21, 26 (cf. Prov. 3:1-4). (IV)

JOHN'S MINISTRY, 3:1-20

The activities of John marked the closing of the period of the law and prophets and the beginning of the period of Jesus (3:21f.). The Jews expected the coming of the kingdom to be preceded by a time of great evil. Israel would need to repent in view of God's impending judgment. To turn from sin would be their acknowledgment of God's just judgment. John came with this word of imminent wrath and a call for change. Because of this he was interpreted as the Messiah (vs. 15). He corrected this misapprehension regarding his person but confirmed the kingdom expectation by pointing to the one who would baptize in the Holy Spirit and fire and would judge.

John's Ministry Introduced, 3:1-6 (Matt. 3:1-6; Mark 1:1-6; John 1:19-23)

[1] John is placed in the context of world history, Jewish history, and prophecy. **The fifteenth year of Tiberius** is usually dated from the death of his predecessor, Augustus, in mid-August of A.D. 14. This would place the opening of John's ministry between mid-August of A.D. 28 and mid-August of A.D. 29. A Jewish method of reckoning his reign would push this date back one year. At this time, or a bit

67

LUKE 3:1, 2 *Roman Rulers*

²in the high-priesthood of Annas and Caiaphas, the word of God came to John the son of Zechariah in the wilderness;

---

later, Jesus was "about thirty" (3:23). This would seem to place the beginning of the Christian era about the year zero, but since other evidence (cited under the comments at 2:1f.) indicates it was earlier, apparently some leeway must be allowed regarding Jesus' exact age, as 3:23 indicates.

Pilate was **governor** from A.D. 26-36. **Judea** had been under direct Roman supervision since A.D. 6, and **Pilate** was fifth in the series of Roman officials who administered the territory.

Herod and **Pilate** were the two of this list of rulers with whom Jesus would be directly concerned. The former was **Herod** Antipas, son of Herod the Great. He ruled Galilee and Perea from 4 B.C.-A.D. 39. He is also mentioned in 3:19; 9:7; 13:31f.; and 23:6f. **Tetrarch,** used only in this verse in the New Testament, first meant a governor of a fourth of an area but later came to refer to a "petty ruler" whose authority was subjected to limitations and dependence on a higher sovereign.

Philip, the best of the Herods (not Philip of Mark 6:14-29), was a half-brother of **Herod** Antipas. Philip ruled his territory from 4 B.C.-A.D. 34. He does not figure subsequently in the gospel. **Ituraea and Trachonitis** were located northeast of Galilee.

Lysanias was given his territory in 4 B.C., according to a Greek inscription found at Abila from the time of Tiberius. **Abilene** was a small region high in the anti-Lebanon mountains north-northeast of Galilee. Luke may mention the last two of these rulers to round out the four areas implied by the original meaning of the word **tetrarch;** or perhaps because they all came to be ruled by Herod Agrippa II, who was Luke's contemporary. (VIII)

[2] Luke names both the important Gentile and Jewish officials of the time. **Annas** had been high priest from A.D.

Jewish Priests **LUKE 3:2, 3**

³ And he went into all the region about the Jordan, preaching a baptism of repentance for the forgiveness of sins.

6/7-A.D. 15 until deposed by Valerius Gratius, Pilate's predecessor. Yet he was still held in high regard by the Jews, and the subsequent high priests were his relatives. So strong was his position that the Jews still considered him high priest, though in the eyes of the Romans he no longer held his office. **Caiaphas,** high priest from about A.D. 18 to about A.D. 36/37, was his son-in-law and played a leading part in the plot against Jesus (Matt. 26:3; John 11:49ff.; 18:13f., 24; cf. Acts 4:6).

After many years, the words regarding John (1:14-17, 76-79) came to pass. In so dating John's appearance Luke marked a significant point of God's actions in history (see Acts 1:22; 10:37; 13:24). John's **word** is described by the Greek term which means a particular utterance, rather than just a general message. (V)

[3] Luke's description of John's itinerary is more extensive than Matthew, who locates the preaching in the wilderness of Judea. Luke uses the word for **baptism** in 3:3; 7:29; 12:50; 20:4; Acts 1:22; 10:37; 13:24; 18:25; and 19:3, 4 (see notes at 3:7). John's immersion of those who came to him would not be a strange practice, since the Jews were familiar with the application of water to the body for ceremonial cleansing. Also, proselytes to Judaism from the Gentile world underwent **a baptism,** which some Jews regarded as a new birth. But **baptism** had not been required of Jews previously, so John's command had significant implications. There was, he indicated, a new necessity for the Israelites to be right with God. This implied the advent of a new era.

John also demanded **repentance.** The noun was a favorite one with Luke, who has over half of the usages of it in the New Testament (3:3, 8; 5:32; 15:7; 24:47; Acts 5:31; 11:18; 20:21; 26:20; and 13:24; 19:4 which both speak of

⁴As it is written in the book of the words of Isaiah
the prophet,
"The voice of one crying in the wilderness:
Prepare the way of the Lord,
make his paths straight.
⁵Every valley shall be filled,
and every mountain and hill shall be brought low,
and the crooked shall be made straight,
and the rough ways shall be made smooth;
⁶and all flesh shall see the salvation of God."

"baptism of repentance"). The same offer of **forgiveness** (see notes at 1:77) was made when the resurrected Christ was first preached (Acts 2:38), but there the gift of the Holy Spirit was an additional benefit.

[4] Luke's quotation, basically the Septuagint of Isaiah 40:3-5, dealt primarily with the return of Israel from Babylonian exile. Here the words are given a Christian application to John. John 1:23 indicates that John the Baptist was responsible for this understanding of the passage. The idea of a **voice in the wilderness** was especially appropriate to the circumstances of his life and ministry. He was to be like a herald, i.e., an officer who would make state or royal proclamations public or who would bear ceremonial messages between authorities. John announced the news of the great King. **Lord** has been changed from "God" in the original, likely to make the selection fit the Messiah. In the Dead Sea Scrolls this passage was applied to the Qumran community (*Manual of Discipline* 8:13f.; 9:19f.). There **the way of the Lord** was prepared by the study of the law and separation from the world.

[5, 6] Luke quotes the Septuagint with minor changes but omits Isaiah 40:5a. Luke's interest in showing the universality of the gospel probably was the reason he extended the quotation through **all flesh**. On **salvation**, see comments at 1:69. (VII, VIII)

Wrath to Come   LUKE 3:7,8

⁷He said therefore to the multitudes that came out to be baptized by him, "You brood of vipers! Who warned you to flee from the wrath to come? ⁸Bear fruits that befit repentance, and do not begin to say to yourselves, 'We have Abraham as our father'; for I tell you, God is able from these stones to raise up children to Abraham.

John's Preaching of Repentance, 3:7-9 (Matt. 3:7-10)

[7] John's popularity shows the people's receptivity and sense of need. The verb for baptize is found elsewhere in 3:12, 16, 21; 7:29, 30; 11:38; and 12:50. Perhaps John used such severe language because he recognized the improper motivation of some who came. They may have come out of curiosity or simply to obey an external act, with no recognition of its internal implications.

John's language was laced with metaphors from the wilderness. The viper was a reptile that inhabited the area. To call the people a viper's **brood** implied that Abraham was not their father and thus purposefully opposed their trust in their ancestry for religious security (verse 8 and see Matt. 12:34; 23:33; the Qumran *Thanksgiving Hymns* 3:17).

The wrath to come has been interpreted by some as the destruction of Jerusalem in A.D. 70, by others as the judgment day, and by others as God's abiding opposition to evil (cf. 21:23; Rom. 1:18; Eph. 5:16; Col. 3:6; 1 Thess. 1:10). (III)

[8] National salvation could come only through a return to righteousness. Otherwise, doom was inevitable. In the coming messianic time Jewish confidence in descent from **Abraham** would be inadequate. Note the Christian rejection of an illicit national confidence in John 8:31-33, 39f.; Romans 2:28f.; 4:13ff.; Galatians 4:21ff. The Qumran community also saw **repentance** (see notes at 3:3) as prerequisite to baptism *(Manual of Discipline* 5:13f.). John may have made his point more impressive by pointing to the **stones** by the

LUKE 3:8-12 — *Fruits of Repentance*

⁹ Even now the axe is laid to the root of the trees; every tree therefore that does not bear good fruit is cut down and thrown into the fire."

¹⁰ And the multitudes asked him, "What then shall we do?" ¹¹ And he answered them, "He who has two coats, let him share with him who has none; and he who has food, let him do likewise." ¹² Tax collectors also came to be baptized, and said to him, "Teacher, what shall we do?"

---

river. If one is correct in assuming the Aramaic expressions he would have used, his language involved a play on the words **stones** (*abanim*) and **children** (*banim*).

[9] **Trees** in the east were valued primarily for fruit and, if barren, were **cut down** (13:6; cf. John 15:6). **Fire** (see also vs. 17) was often used as a symbol of judgment (Matt. 7:19; 13:40-42). Even if judgment had been deferred previously, now it was sure. (III)

John's Preaching to Special Groups, 3:10-14

[10] Verses 10-14 expand the idea of the "fruits of repentance" of verse 8. Luke turns to those who responded positively to John. Each group was asked to forsake its besetting sin, and all were told to do their duty to their neighbor. John was, in effect, telling them to let the conditions of the kingdom be realized in them. These were the exhibitions of just behavior that Jews associated with the kingdom.

[11] Here again is Luke's concern with the poor and needy. The coat (*chitōn*) was the under garment, as distinguished from the upper one (cf. 9:3; Matt. 10:10). Nothing is said about an abundance of **food.** They were simply to **share** what they had.

[12, 13] The **tax collectors** were Jewish underlings who did the actual gathering of taxes for their Roman employers, who in turn had made a contract with the government to do the collecting (see other references at 5:27-32; 7:34; 15:1f.; 18:9-14; and 19:1-10). These Jews were despised by their

Tax Collectors   LUKE 3:12-16

¹³And he said to them, "Collect no more than is appointed you." ¹⁴Soldiers also asked him, "And we, what shall we do?" And he said to them, "Rob no one by violence or by false accusation, and be content with your wages."

¹⁵As the people were in expectation, and all men questioned in their hearts concerning John, whether perhaps he was the Christ, ¹⁶John answered them all, "I baptize you with water;

---

countrymen, both because the Roman tax was unpopular and because they would often resort to extortionate methods in order to gain a greater dividend for themselves. It was unusual that such people would even come to hear John, but this indicates something of the moral sensibility even they had (Matt. 21:31f.). The title **"teacher"** was equivalent to "Rabbi," according to an inscription on a first-century Jewish tomb. John did not condemn them for doing their job but only insisted they not abuse it. On baptism, see notes at 3:7.

[14] These would be Jewish **soldiers,** perhaps police. They may have helped the tax collectors in intimidating the people, likely for a part of the unjustly gotten gain.

John's Messianic Preaching, 3:15-18 (Matt. 3:11f.; Mark 1:7f.)

[15] Various alleged Christs kept messianic hopes high. But **John,** whose actions were those that would herald the messianic age (see comments prior to 3:1), especially raised them. Yet John was an enigma. Though a sign of the messianic era, he himself bore none of the insignia of royalty and was not of Davidic descent (cf. John 1:24-28; 3:28). On **Christ** see notes at 2:11. Luke shows more clearly than do Matthew and Mark the intensity of the popular reactions (see John 1:19-22).

[16] It was apparently by revelation that John had received this information. Use of the present participle

LUKE 3:16, 17 — Baptism With Fire

but he who is mightier than I is coming, the thong of whose sandals I am not worthy to untie; he will baptize you with the Holy Spirit and with fire. ¹⁷His winnowing fork is in his hand, to clear his threshing floor, and to gather the wheat into his granary, but the chaff he will burn with unquenchable fire."

---

coming indicates the process was already under way. A slave would unfasten his master's shoes when he arrived home. **John** felt himself even unworthy for that menial task when the **mightier** one came (yet see John 13:5). One of John's great virtues was his humility in accepting the role God had assigned him.

Jesus would bring a new baptism. John stated the nature of it, but not the purpose. It was to involve, apparently, more than just the remission of sins which John offered (see Acts 1:5; 10:44; 11:16; and 19:4). The baptism of **the Holy Spirit** was obviously fulfilled on Pentecost (Acts 2:1-4), as prophesied in Joel 2:28ff. Several explanations of **fire** have been offered. One is the fiery tongues of Pentecost, making **Holy Spirit and fire** both relate to the act of God on that day. Another is that there were two baptisms, and **fire** was the judgment of the impenitent (cf. vs. 17). Another is that the **fire** refers to purification which the Messiah's baptism would bring by grace. Yet John's baptism also offered purification or remission. Others think the reference was to fiery trials of persecution (see 12:50-53; Mark 10:38f.). On **Holy Spirit,** notes 1:15; baptism, 3:7. (VI)

[17] This verse unquestionably refers to judgment, and opinions have differed as to whether this **fire** is the same as that in verse 16. **Winnowing** was done in the later afternoon or evening, when the wind was blowing. The **fork** was a fan-like shovel used to throw the grain into the air so the wind would blow away **the chaff.** In addition, **the chaff** here was also burned. The **fire** would be one so fierce it could not be extinguished, rather than one that would never go out (cf. Mark 9:43). (III, IV, VII)

John Imprisoned LUKE 3:18-20

¹⁸ So, with many other exhortations, he preached good news to the people. ¹⁹ But Herod the tetrarch, who had been reproved by him for Herodias, his brother's wife, and for all the evil things that Herod had done, ²⁰ added this to them all, that he shut up John in prison.

---

[18] The **good news** (see notes at 1:19) would be the message of forgiveness (verse 3) and the advent of a new relationship between God and man (verses 15-17). This verse confirms the opinion that Luke gives us a summary of the teaching of John rather than a verbatim account of what happened on a given occasion.

John's Imprisonment, 3:19, 20 (Matt. 14:3-12; Mark 6:17-30)

[19] It was quite courageous for John to extend his judgment by preaching even to the ruler. **Herod** had stolen the **wife** of his brother Philip (not the tetrarch of 3:1). Only Luke notes that John also condemned the man's other wickednesses. (V, VI)

[20] Josephus (*Antiquities* XVIII, v, 3) said Herod imprisoned **John** because he was afraid John's popularity might lead the people to revolt. Josephus likely gave Herod's public reasons for the arrest, whereas Luke gives Herod's private ones. **John** was imprisoned at Machaerus at the northeast corner of the Dead Sea and, ironically, near the area where he had spent a good part of his life.

As previously (1:56), Luke finishes this story before moving on to another. Luke later makes brief allusion to the death of **John** (9:7-9).

THE RESPONSE OF JESUS: INAUGURATION AND PREPARATION, 3:21—4:13

This section presents Jesus in several perspectives. His baptism, and especially the descent of the Spirit, were an

LUKE 3:21, 22 — *Jesus Baptized*

[21] Now when all the people were baptized, and when Jesus also had been baptized and was praying, the heaven was opened, **[22]** and the Holy Spirit descended upon him in bodily

---

inauguration and introduced his life as Spirit led—an idea developed further in 4:14f., 16-30. The genealogy traces Jesus' kinship with all humanity through Adam. The temptation furthers this identification with humanity. These three paragraphs share the idea of Jesus as the Son of God (3:22, 38; 4:3, 9). He is the God-approved and Spirit-empowered man (3:22; 4:1f.) who brings good news (see 4:14-30). The identity of Jesus will be developed more fully in chapters 4:14-9:51 (note, e.g., 4:34, 41; 5:24).

The Baptism of Jesus, 3:21, 22 (Matt. 3:13-17; Mark 1:9-11; cf. John 1:29-34)

[21] This event formed a climax to John's baptismal ministry. Now Jesus would embark on his ministry. The gospels do not, of course, associate Jesus' baptism with remission of sins, even though at the time of the baptism the people would not have known Jesus as sinless. Matthew 3:15 says it was to "fulfill all righteousness." Jesus was accepting what God was doing in inaugurating the kingdom and his baptism was an indication of the rightness of God's actions through John. His response was a focal point of John's work. Significant, too, was the heavenly announcement and the descent of the Holy Spirit. Then, in his baptism Jesus identified himself with the people he came to save.

Only Luke records that Jesus prayed when he was **baptized,** and this is a significant element in Luke's understanding of prayer. It was as a man of prayer that Jesus was thus set apart by God (see notes at 1:10).

[22] This verse is the focal point of Luke's record (cf. John 1:33f.; also "my Father" in Luke 2:49). The heavenly

Beloved Son   LUKE 3:22, 23

form, as a dove, and a voice came from heaven, "Thou art my beloved Son;[j] with thee I am well pleased."[k]

[23] Jesus, when he began his ministry, was about thirty years of age, being the son (as was supposed) of Joseph, the son of Heli,

[j] Or *my Son, my* (or *the*) *Beloved*
[k] Other ancient authorities read *today I have begotten thee*

---

words derive from Isaiah 42:1, referring to the servant of the Lord, and Psalm 2:7, referring to the divinely chosen king. In the latter passage the king was opposed by the nations but was vindicated by God who dwells above all earthly sovereigns. So it would be the case with Jesus (see Acts 4:25f.). In the Old Testament the expression "**Son of God**" was used of angels (Job 1:6), the nation (Ex. 4:22), and the king (2 Sam. 7:14). In later Judaism the term was used of the Messiah (*4 Ezra* 7:28), which is the sense here (see notes at 1:35). Some Greek texts have here "today I have begotten thee," doubtless under the influence of Psalm 2:7. On the word **beloved** see 9:35; 20:13. The revelatory announcement here formed the inaugural to the ministry of the servant king. **The Holy Spirit** was his anointing for his task (see notes at 1:15). (IV, VI) It is worth noting that the disciple, as Jesus, receives the **Holy Spirit** at baptism (Acts 2:38) and is declared a son (Gal. 3:26f.).

The Genealogy of Jesus, 3:23-38 (Matt. 1:1-16)

[23] Jesus' **age** as given here is approximate (see discussion at 3:1f.). **Jesus** began his work at the same **age** King David had begun his (2 Sam. 5:4).

Luke's genealogy differs from Matthew's in length, arrangement, and in many of the names. Luke has his at this point in the gospel, rather than at the beginning (as did Matthew), because he wishes to attach Jesus' genealogy to the beginning of **his ministry** (cf. Ex. 6:14-25). There have been many approaches to reconciling Matthew and Luke ever since the problem was first considered ca. A.D. 200.

²⁴the son of Matthat, the son of Levi, the son of Melchi, the son of Jannai, the son of Joseph, ²⁵the son of Mattathias, the son of Amos, the son of Nahum, the son of Esli, the son of Naggai, ²⁶the son of Maath, the son of Mattathias, the son of Semein, the son of Josech, the son of Joda, ²⁷the son of Joanan, the son of Rhesa, the son of Zerubbabel, the son of Shealtiel,¹ the son of Neri, ²⁸the son of Melchi, the son of Addi, the son of Cosam, the son of Elmadam, the son of Er, ²⁹the son of Joshua, the son of Eliezer, the son of Jorim, the son of Matthat, the son of Levi,

¹Greek *Salathiel*

They include suppositions of levirate marriages, opinions that the two lines were given from different viewpoints (e.g., legal and actual), or that both the lines of Mary and Joseph are given (cf. 4:22; John 1:45; 6:42). These attempts show that reconciliation is possible, though no one answer is acceptable to all. For further genealogical material see Genesis 5:3-32; 11:10-26; Ruth 4:18-22; 1 Chronicles 1:1-4, 24-28; 2:1-15.

[24-27] In this list of names Matthew and Luke meet only at **Zerubbabel** and **Shealtiel**. The names Luke gives are unknown apart from this account. **Zerubbabel** was probably **the real son** of Pediah, and nephew of **Shealtiel** (1 Chron. 3:17-19), who became the heir of **Shealtiel,** who had no sons. **Shealtiel,** in turn, was called in Matthew 1:12 and 1 Chronicles 3:17 the son of Jechoniah, whereas here he is **the son of Neri.** Jechoniah was childless (Jer. 22:30), so in him David's line through Solomon ended. Then his heir seems to have become **Shealtiel,** who was of David's line through Nathan (yet see Ezra 3:2, which may have been Luke's source).

[28-38] With slight additions in Luke, this list coincides with Matthew as far as **Abraham.** By linking Jesus with God's original creation, Luke shows his interest in all humanity, as Matthew shows his special Jewish interest by going back only so far as **Abraham.** Thus, Luke is saying

Genealogy   LUKE 3:28—4:2

[30] the son of Simeon, the son of Judah, the son of Joseph, the son of Jonam, the son of Eliakim, [31] the son of Melea, the son of Menna, the son of Mattatha, the son of Nathan, the son of David, [32] the son of Jesse, the son of Obed, the son of Boaz, the son of Sala, the son of Nahshon, [33] the son of Amminadab, the son of Admin, the son of Arni, the son of Hezron, the son of Perez, the son of Judah, [34] the son of Jacob, the son of Isaac, the son of Abraham, the son of Terah, the son of Nahor, [35] the son of Serug, the son of Reu, the son of Peleg, the son of Eber, the son of Shelah, [36] the son of Cainan, the son of Arphaxad, the son of Shem, the son of Noah, the son of Lamech, [37] the son of Methuselah, the son of Enoch, the son of Jared, the son of Mahalaleel, the son of Cainan, [38] the son of Enos, the son of Seth, the son of Adam, the son of God.

[1] And Jesus, full of the Holy Spirit, returned from the Jordan, and was led by the Spirit [2] for forty days in the wilderness, tempted by the devil. And he ate nothing in those days; and when they were ended, he was hungry.

---

that all mankind can consider the Messiah as brother (cf. 1 Cor. 3:23). **Adam**, the first man, is called a **son of God**, perhaps as a reminder that the human race was of divine origin but, more significantly, to demonstrate a way in which Jesus was a **son of God** and, in a sense, a second **Adam** (cf. 23:43). (IV, VIII)

The Temptations of Jesus, 4:1-13 (Matt. 4:1-11; Mark 1:12f.)

[1] **The Spirit** (see 3:22; and notes at 1:15) assured **Jesus** of God's presence and help. All of the Synoptic Gospels note that Jesus was **led by the Spirit,** but only Luke has the expression **full of the Holy Spirit** (see also Acts 2:4; 6:3, 5; 7:55; 11:24).

[2] The **forty** day period may have preceded the temptations, or the three temptations may be representative of struggles which continued throughout the whole period. On the number **forty,** compare the fasts of Moses and Elijah

LUKE 4:2-4 — *The Devil*

³The devil said to him, "If you are the Son of God, command this stone to become bread." ⁴And Jesus answered him, "It is written, 'Man shall not live by bread alone.'"

(Ex. 34:28; Deut. 9:9; 1 Kings 19:8; and cf. Lev. 12:1-4; Ezek. 4:6; 29:11).

Jesus was led out to be **tempted** (Matt. 4:1). **In the wilderness** (in contrast to "into" in Matthew and Mark) indicates it was in the Spirit's strength (cf. verse 1) that he overcame—i.e., he was led by the Spirit through the total experience. In this and the next two stories (4:14-30) Jesus' ministry is explained by the Spirit's power (cf. 3:21f.). Here his sinlessness is Spirit-aided. **Tempted** here indicates to "try" or "test," in order to produce perplexity or failure, i.e., sin.

This is the first reference to **the devil** in Luke. Other references are in 4:3, 6, 13; and 8:12. See also the references to Satan, listed at 10:18. In the temptation episode, both Jesus and **the devil** presuppose Jesus' messiahship and divine sonship (verse 3), the authority of scripture to reveal God's will (vss. 4, 10ff.), and the lordship of Satan over the present age (vs. 6). The temptations were to make Jesus "prove" his messiahship and, therefore, to pervert it.

[3] The devil attacked a point of special susceptibility—Jesus' hunger. The challenge called upon Jesus to employ his divine sonship to alleviate physical need. The thing in itself was not wrong and was within Jesus' power. But this was not the role of **the Son of God** (see notes at 1:35). Nor would he do his first wonder at the behest of and in league with such an ally. Jesus overcame the ever present temptation to put material things ahead of spiritual, and therefore so can his followers. (IV)

[4] Christ did not defend his divine sonship; rather he gave an answer good for any child of God in similar temptation. His answer was a verbatim quotation of Deuteronomy 8:3b from the Septuagint. The Old Testament context described God's provision of manna, perhaps implying that **Jesus** meant, "God cared for Israel, and will care for me."

World's Kingdoms — LUKE 4:5-8

⁵And the devil took him up, and showed him all the kingdoms of the world in a moment of time, ⁶and said to him, "To you I will give all this authority and their glory; for it has been delivered to me, and I give it to whom I will. ⁷If you, then, will worship me, it shall all be yours." ⁸And Jesus answered him, "It is written, 'You shall worship the Lord your God, and him only shall you serve.' "

Further, Jesus did not come to supply **bread** for humanity but to answer their deeper needs.

[5] Luke has the second and third temptations in the reverse of Matthew's order. One cannot know the original order, but the content is the important element. Matthew indicates that the event was on a very high mountain. This was probably a visionary experience rather than a case of bodily transport, since Satan would not have control of the movement of Jesus' body and since there was no one physical locale from which all the world's **kingdoms** could be seen.

[6] Only Luke records Satan's statement about the world being his (cf. 4:2; 10:18). The world may have been given the devil by God's permission or by man's sins (cf. Matt. 8:29; John 12:31; 14:30; 16:11; Eph. 2:2; 1 John 3:8; 5:19; Rev. 13:2, 4). Yet ultimately it would not be his, but God's. Thus Jesus could refuse, knowing that he would one day have the world on his, not Satan's terms. It may be that the devil was offering to promote the messianic kingdom if the Messiah would follow him. Or he may have been influencing Jesus to be a political Messiah, a task which the Lord repudiated throughout his ministry. In any event, to accept the devil's support in the kingdom activities would be to defeat the inner nature of the kingdom. **Authority** is found elsewhere in Luke 4:32, 36; 5:24; 7:8; 9:1; 10:19; 12:5, 11; 19:17; 20:2, 8, 20; 22:53; 23:7.

[7] **Worship** would acknowledge the devil had ultimate power over the world, which was not true (see Dan. 5:21). Thus, ultimately, it was not his to give.

[8] Jesus, by quoting Deuteronomy 6:13f., rejected the

⁹And he took him to Jerusalem, and set him on the pinnacle of the temple, and said to him, "If you are the Son of God, throw yourself down from here; ¹⁰for it is written,

'He will give his angels charge of you,
to guard you,'

¹¹and

'On their hands they will bear you up,
lest you strike your foot against a stone.' "

¹²And Jesus answered him, "It is said, 'You shall not tempt the Lord your God.' "

---

pathway of political messiahship, which led many Jews to reject him. The context of the Old Testament passage was the entry into Canaan and the need to avoid entanglements with foreign deities. Israel was to remember the true source of her blessings. Here, the kingdoms could ultimately only be God's to bestow. Satan had usurped his authority, and the rebellion must be put down.

[9] Luke places the temptation regarding **Jerusalem** in the climactic place, in accord with his special emphasis on the city (see notes at 2:22). As in the first temptation, Jesus' faith as **the Son of God** was again challenged (see verse 3). As before, this may have been a visionary experience (cf. Ezek. 8:3). (IV)

[10, 11] Here, for the first time, Satan used scripture. Psalm 91:11f. was given a messianic interpretation by the rabbis. Jesus did not argue about Satan's use of the passage, since that was not the basic conflict. The temptation asked Jesus to create a danger, whereas in the first temptation the crisis (hunger) already existed. It was as if Satan said, "You will not know about yourself, and the veracity of God's promise, till you test it." On **angels,** see notes at 1:11. (VII)

[12] For the third time **Jesus** responded with scripture. Deuteronomy 6:16 referred to Israel's tempting **God** at Massah. Simply put, **Jesus** was saying that tempting **God** is not

Temptation Overcome   LUKE 4:12, 13

[13] And when the devil had ended every temptation, he departed from him until an opportune time.

---

trusting him (see 1 Cor. 10:9; but cf. Isa. 7:12). There was no purpose to be served by yielding to the temptation.

[13] It has been pointed out that what happened to Jesus can be paralleled to the avenues of **temptation** set forth in 1 John 2:14-17 and to the original temptation of Genesis 3:6. Perhaps this story is saying that Jesus was tempted through all the avenues by which man can be tempted (see Heb. 4:15). Satan **departed**, but not for good (22:3). On **the devil**, see notes at 4:2; 10:18. (VI, VIII)

Following this story, Luke records three miracles, showing that Jesus did have messianic power. They are found in reverse order to the temptations. The threat at the brow of the hill (4:29) corresponds to the pinnacle temptation; the expulsion of the demon (4:35f.) to the desire of Satan for Jesus' worship; and the catch of fishes (5:6) to the bread temptation.

IV

The Galilean Ministry, 4:14 — 9:50

THE EARLY MINISTRY, 4:14—6:11

THIS SECTION SHOWS Jesus as he moved into his ministry, and the "period of the Lord" really begins. He is the Spirit-empowered teacher (4:14f.; cf. 4:43) and healer (4:18f.) who fulfills God's messianic intent (4:21). Several factors are stressed in 4:14—6:11. Prominent are the reactions to Jesus, from the rejection at Nazareth (4:29) to the fury in the synagogue (6:11), with varied reactions between. The acceptance and rejection theme of the gospel is fully introduced here. (VI) Also Jesus' authority is introduced in teaching (4:32), over demons (4:35), over disease (4:39; 5:13, 24), and over the religious traditions (5:36-39; 6:1-11). The reader is called upon to consider the claim of such a figure. Yet in all this the content of Jesus' teachings remains a relative secret from Luke's readers. The section focuses on who Jesus is and how people respond to him. The next division (esp. 6:17-49) will set forth his teachings in detail. (VI, VIII)

The First Preaching in Galilee, 4:14, 15 (Matt. 4:12-17; Mark 1:14f.)

[14] Though the gospel of John indicates an early ministry in Judea, in the Synoptics the preaching began in **Galilee,**

First Preaching **LUKE 4:14-16**

¹⁴ And Jesus returned in the power of the Spirit into Galilee, and a report concerning him went through all the surrounding country. ¹⁵ And he taught in their synagogues, being glorified by all.

¹⁶ And he came to Nazareth, where he had been brought up; and he went to the synagogue, as his custom was, on the sabbath day. And he stood up to read;

---

and here Jesus' reputation began to spread. Luke wants his readers to recognize the source of Jesus' power (see notes at 1:17; see 3:22; 4:1, 2, 18; cf. also 6:19), so he points out that Jesus' preaching and his healing (see 4:18) were Spirit impelled activities (1:15). Thus, as these activities are depicted in the remainder of the gospel, the reader knows the power by which they were accomplished.

[15] This note is followed by two supporting synagogue incidents (16-30, 31-37). In them Luke stresses the reactions to Jesus. The concept of glorification is frequent in Luke (notes, 2:20). Here one is shown the early popularity of Jesus before rejection crystallized (but note vs. 29). (IV, VI)

The Rejection at Nazareth, 4:16-30 (Matt. 13:53-58; Mark 6:1-6)

[16] Here is the first of several **sabbath** incidents in this section of Luke (4:31-37; 38f.; 40f.; 6:1-11; see other references to the **sabbath** in 13:10, 14, 15, 16; 14:1, 3, 5; 23:54, 56; 24:1).

Luke first stresses the character and work of Jesus and later begins to emphasize the teaching (4:43, and especially beginning in 6:20, but see 4:21). Also Luke notes the early reactions to Jesus and draws an interesting contrast by following his praise (4:15) with a rejection story. Notice that both the Galilean (present text) and non-Galilean (9:51-56) ministries begin with rejection.

The implication of the words **brought up** here, and of

LUKE 4:16-19 *Synagogue Reading*

[17] and there was given to him the book of the prophet Isaiah. He opened the book and found the place where it was written,
[18] "The Spirit of the Lord is upon me,
because he has anointed me to preach
good news to the poor.
He has sent me to proclaim release
to the captives
and recovering of sight to the blind,
to set at liberty those who are
oppressed,
[19] to proclaim the acceptable year of
the Lord."

4:23, is that Jesus had not lived at **Nazareth** for some time. He would be the same person they had known before, but he had had some remarkable experiences and had gone through some changes since they had last seen him.

Jesus was either asked **to read** or **stood,** indicating his desire to do so. The usual custom was to stand while reading and to sit when commenting (vs. 20; Matt. 5:1; Mark 4:1; John 8:2; but note a different procedure in Acts 13:16). The lesson was read in Hebrew, with the subsequent interpretation in Aramaic or Greek.

[17] Some suggest there may have been a lectionary cycle at this time, and the text was the one due for that day. That would explain why a scripture so far into the scroll (**the book** form was not yet in use) would be read. If Jesus, on the other hand, unrolled the scroll all the way to the passage (Isa. 61:1f.), it would impress the people that he would take such pains to read that particular text.

[18, 19] This reference indicates Jesus' understanding of the task to which he was committed. **The Spirit** was the power in which Jesus would carry on his healing ministry, as with the teaching ministry in 4:14f. (on Holy **Spirit,** see notes at 1:15). Isaiah 61:1f. resembled the servant songs in Isaiah (chapters 42-53). It also used language similar to

Jesus' Ministry   LUKE 4:18-20

[20] And he closed the book, and gave it back to the attendant, and sat down; and the eyes of all in the synagogue were fixed on him.

---

that describing the year of Jubilee (Lev. 25), though identification with that event seems doubtful because of some differences in detail between Leviticus and Isaiah. The text is a rather loose quotation of the Septuagint. For a similar phenomenon see Matthew 15:8; Acts 7:37; and Romans 13:9. The last phrase of verse 18 is an insertion from Isaiah 58:6. The question is whether this was the work of Jesus or the work of Luke, who adds his own comment regarding the Lord's ministry.

Here again one sees Luke's interest in **the poor.** The Greek term always had a bad meaning prior to the gospels, implying abject poverty. Yet here it most likely suggests those who were receptive to the gospel (see 6:20; 7:22; 14:13, 21; 16:20, 22; 18:22; 19:8; 21:3; cf. also Isa. 57:15; 1 Cor. 1:27f.; James 2:5).

These blessings were both spiritual and physical. **Captives** were, literally, prisoners of war. **Release** is the same word elsewhere translated forgiveness (see notes at 1:77). Perhaps **the blind, poor,** etc. were to be taken symbolically, not literally, though Jesus also rendered literal help in certain of these areas. **The acceptable year** was apparently the time when the Lord would act to do the things described, i.e., a day of the Messiah, which would be God's great time for blessing his people (cf. 2 Cor. 6:2). On the idea of anointing, see Acts 4:27; 10:38. On **proclaim** see notes at 1:19. (I, II, VII)

[20] Actually Jesus would roll up the scroll, rather than close **the book** (see vs. 17). The **attendant** (from a word meaning, literally, an "under-rower"), is usually thought to be the *chazzan,* a synagogue functionary. The expectation of the people was because teaching came at this point (cf. Acts 3:4; 6:15). (VI)

LUKE 4:21-23   *Isaiah Fulfilled*

²¹And he began to say to them, "Today this scripture has been fulfilled in your hearing." ²²And all spoke well of him, and wondered at the gracious words which proceeded out of his mouth; and they said, "Is not this Joseph's son?" ²³And he said to them, "Doubtless you will quote to me this proverb, 'Physician, heal yourself; what we have heard you did at Capernaum, do here also in your own country.'"

---

[21] Jesus' claim was audacious. He was saying the messianic age had come and was implying that he himself fulfilled the messianic expectation (cf. Matt. 5:17; 2 Cor. 6:2). In Matthew 11:2-6 and Luke 7:22 Jesus clearly applied Isaiah 61 to himself. He argued that since he was the worker of the signs, he must be the Messiah. Having rejected false conceptions of messiahship in the temptation, Jesus now set forth the proper view of the messianic mission. (IV, VII)

[22] It must have been a great surprise that someone who was reared in Nazareth would say such things. After all, Joseph was a common, uneducated man. Where had his son acquired such information? **All spoke well of him** could refer to the initial reaction of those in the synagogue, or it could be a general description of his reputation prior to these events which precipitated his rejection. The question of the people may well summarize the general skepticism of the Nazarenes, and the doubt thereby implied may be what spurred Jesus' further remarks.

[23] Luke has not recorded any of Jesus' miracles to this point (the first is in 4:33ff.), but they had apparently been worked (on miracles in **Capernaum** see 4:31-35, 40f.; 7:1-10). Jesus may have been responding to the remark in verse 22, but more probably it was to previous complaints. Also, it must be remembered that he often showed knowledge of men's thoughts. (III) Hence the **proverb,** which in its original form was probably "Heal your own lameness." The implication of Jesus' statement was that the Nazarenes

Capernaum LUKE 4:23-26

²⁴ And he said, "Truly, I say to you, no prophet is acceptable in his own country. ²⁵ But in truth, I tell you, there were many widows in Israel in the days of Elijah, when the heaven was shut up three years and six months, when there came a great famine over all the land; ²⁶ and Elijah was sent to none of them but only to Zarephath, in the land of Sidon, to a woman who was a widow.

---

claimed they would believe only after they had seen the signs. (On other requests for a sign see 4:3; 11:16; 22:64; 23:8, 35ff.) But Jesus reversed the order: there had been no signs because they were a faithless people. He illustrated by reference to faithless Israel in the Old Testament—a comparison that would have telling effect on his hearers.

There is a puzzle as to when Jesus moved to **Capernaum.** Matthew 4:13 indicates he had already moved there, whereas Luke 4:31 indicates it was after this incident. Luke may not be chronological but has put this incident at the beginning of the ministry in order to delineate its character and its reception by the people. (IV)

[24] This saying, probably also proverbial (see John 4:44), explained the reason for his previous remark. **Truly** is from the Greek form of "amen" (see 9:27; 12:44; 21:3). The material following this general statement flowed from it and implied from Israel's history what sort of people those of Nazareth were. They were unbelievers, and Jesus would not work a sign to gratify them. Also Jesus here saw himself as a **prophet,** in addition to his previous reference to himself as anointed by the Spirit (4:18ff.). (VI)

[25, 26] The story of **Elijah** is found in 1 Kings 17 and 18. In 1 Kings 18:1 it is said the rain came in the third year, in contrast to the **three years and six months** of Luke. Perhaps Luke also included the time of famine, which would be longer than the drought (see also James 5:17). **Israel,** because of not receiving a prophet, was denied blessing, which went to a Gentile who was receptive. (VIII)

²⁷And there were many lepers in Israel in the time of the prophet Elisha; and none of them was cleansed, but only Naaman the Syrian." ²⁸When they heard this, all in the synagogue were filled with wrath. ²⁹And they rose up and put him out of the city, and led him to the brow of the hill on which their city was built, that they might throw him down headlong.

---

[27] Jesus made the same point with the second illustration (see 2 Kings 5:1-14). Part of the offense to Jesus' listeners was the implication that they were not as worthy of God's blessings as a Gentile. It was shocking enough to be told of their disbelief, but such comparisons as this, with the possible implication that Jesus might eventually go to Gentiles, would be even more upsetting and explain their subsequent wrath. (III, VIII)

[28] Their **wrath** may have been because of his condemnation of their faithlessness; or because of his implicit acceptance of Gentiles; or because of Jesus' claims for himself (anointed one, prophet, equal to Elijah and Elisha); or for other reasons. The charges would be even harder to accept from someone who had grown up in Nazareth.

[29] This was violent treatment (cf. John 8:59; 10:31), especially considering that the first rejection of Jesus noted by Luke comes from those who logically might be expected to accept him (cf. Matt. 23:37). Some suggest this was the form of punishment known as "the rebel's beating," which was analogous to lynch law. It was administered by the people, without trial and on the spot, to one caught in what was felt to be a flagrant violation of the law or tradition. Or, if this were a stoning (*Sanhedrin* 6:4a), it would imply that the people thought Jesus guilty of blasphemy. This event was a harbinger of the persecution Jesus would suffer in his later ministry.

There is some difficulty in locating a **brow** upon which Nazareth was built. **The city** was located on a hollow high

Miracle Stories   LUKE 4:29-32

³⁰ But passing through the midst of them he went away. ³¹ And he went down to Capernaum, a city of Galilee. And he was teaching them on the sabbath; ³² and they were astonished at his teaching, for his word was with authority.

---

against the slopes of a mountain and was enclosed on three sides by more elevated sides of the mountain. (VI)

[30] It is difficult to determine if this were meant as a miracle or not (cf. John 10:39). It seems hard to explain Jesus' escape unless there was so much confusion that he slipped away. Jesus' death would not come till the appointed time (13:31-34). This story forms a sort of prologue to the later time when Jesus would be taken outside Jerusalem and actually killed on a hill. Even then he escaped from death's bonds. (IV)

Jesus in the Synagogue at Capernaum, 4:31-37 (Mark 1:21-28; cf. also Matt. 7:28f.)

[31] From this point through 5:26 Luke gives a series of miracle stories, showing Jesus' power and authority. However, more emphasis is given the reactions to these works than to the way they were done (see 4:36f., 41f.; 5:11, 15, 25f.).

This is Luke's second consecutive **sabbath** story, though this healing did not evoke criticism in contrast to later **sabbath** activities (6:1-11). The contrast between this healing and those controversies affords a good index to the changing reactions to Jesus.

Capernaum was the chief Jewish town of the neighborhood (northwest corner of Sea of Galilee) and therefore a good center for Jesus' operations. Its description as **a city of Galilee** was probably for Luke's Gentile readers, who would need such identification. In contrast to his refusal in Nazareth, in **Capernaum** Jesus did a sign.

[32] Jesus' **authority** shows something of his impact on

LUKE 4:32-34   *Demons*

³³ And in the synagogue there was a man who had the spirit of an unclean demon; and he cried out with a loud voice, ³⁴ "Ah!ᵐ What have you to do with us, Jesus of Nazareth? Have you come here to destroy us? I know who you are, the Holy One of God."

   ᵐ Or *let us alone*.

---

those who heard (see notes at 4:6). He did not need to rely on external testimony to verify his message (cf. Mt. 5; 7:28f.). (IV, VI)

[33] The reaction **in the** Capernaum **synagogue** contrasts markedly with that in Nazareth. Here even the **demon**, unlike the Nazarenes, believed, and a sign was done.

This is the first reference to a **demon** in Luke (other instances are 4:41; 6:18; 7:21; 8:27-39; 9:1, 37-43, 49f.; 10:17; 11:14, 19f., 24f.; and perhaps 13:10-17). Demons were malign spiritual beings who could inhabit corporeal bodies with varying catastrophic results. Men were in a helpless dread of them. That was why Jesus' power over them was so impressive. Such victories were lesser skirmishes in the overall struggle with evil's supreme embodiment, Satan (see vs. 35). The emphasis of this story is on the confrontation with evil, even more than on the healing. **The spirit of** may simply mean an influence belonging to **an unclean demon.** Some feel that **unclean** indicated that the possessed man was kept from the worship of God, as if he had some sore of ceremonial uncleanness.

The man's specific malady is unknown. It was unusual that he was **in the synagogue.** Perhaps he came unobserved, or perhaps his distress had lain dormant till the presence of Jesus had forced a crisis and evil declared itself.

[34] Notice the interchangeable use of the singular and plural (**he, I,** and **us**). The spirit seemed to speak through the human vocal mechanism so that both singular and plural could be used. The question meant, "what have we in common?" The spirit seemed to fear **Jesus.**

Holy One of God is only here, Mark 1:24, and John 6:69.

An Exorcism   LUKE 4:34-36

³⁵But Jesus rebuked him, saying, "Be silent, and come out of him!" And when the demon had thrown him down in the midst, he came out of him, having done him no harm. ³⁶And they were all amazed and said to one another, "What is this word? For with authority and power he commands the unclean spirits and they come out."

This statement was doubtless a messianic designation and is incorporated by Luke as he unfolds Jesus' identity (see John 6:69; and cf. Matt. 16:16). It is significant that **Jesus** was recognized by an unclean spirit, when his own kinsmen at Nazareth would not recognize him (cf. James 2:19). Perhaps demonic recognition was meant as contrasting testimony to the tragedy of man's unbelief. (VI)

[35] According to Jewish tradition demonic power was to be crushed when the messianic age came (cf. *Test. Zebulun* 9:8). Thus this act was a sign (see 2:12). **Jesus,** using a verb often used of rebuking violence, told the spirit to **be silent** or, literally, "be muzzled." Rebuke is found also in 4:39, 41; 8:24; 9:21, 42, 55; 17:3; 18:5, 39; 19:39; 23:40. **Jesus** may have forbidden the spirit to speak because he did not wish public recognition from such a source. People could conceivably link his power with the demon's. Nor did **Jesus** wish, at that point, to make a full self-revelation. (I)

Though **the demon** could control his victim physically, he was compelled to obey Jesus' word of command. The fact the man was unharmed was probably mentioned because it was unusual. The convulsions and loud cry would make the spectators expect **harm** to have been done. (V)

[36] The audience in Mark asked if Jesus had "a new teaching" (1:27). Here his deeds, as well as his words (32) were authoritative (see notes at 4:32). The **amazed** onlookers apparently had not heard of Jesus' exorcising before. Too, he did it with a **word,** eschewing any elaborate techniques. **Power,** used here, was a favorite word with Luke (see notes at 1:17). (IV,VI)

LUKE 4:37-39 — *Peter's Mother-in-Law*

³⁷ And reports of him went out into every place in the surrounding region.

³⁸ And he arose and left the synagogue, and entered Simon's house. Now Simon's mother-in-law was ill with a high fever, and they besought him for her. ³⁹ And he stood over her and rebuked the fever, and it left her; and immediately she rose and served them.

---

[37] This verse is similar to 4:14f. (see also 5:15), so Luke here has a small synagogue section in verses 14-37, with an opening and closing formula. Verses 16-37 are an expansion of the "heading" in verses 14f. (IV, VI)

The Healing of Peter's Mother-in-Law, 4:38, 39 (Matt. 8:14f.; Mark 1:29-31)

[38] According to Mark, James and John were present at this event. However, they have not yet been introduced in Luke (see 5:1-11—the events are not necessarily in chronological order). Luke adds drama by indicating **they besought** Jesus, whereas Mark simply says they told Jesus of **her**.

This is the first introduction to Simon in Luke. Yet he is treated as a person who would be familiar to the readers, as was his family situation. Simon, who apparently lived in Capernaum, had formerly dwelt in the nearby town of Bethsaida (John 1:44). The name Simon is found in 5:3, 4, 5, 8, 10; 6:14; 22:31; and 24:34; and Peter is in 5:8, 6:14; 8:45, 51; 9:20, 28, 32, 33; 12:41; 18:28; 22:8, 34, 54, 55, 58, 60, 61; 24:12.

It has been contended that this was **Simon's** step-mother. However, if that were the case, the Greek would have used a different term. Only Luke describes her **fever** as **high** (in contrast to slight fevers), perhaps indicating medical precision. (VI)

[39] Only Luke emphasizes how suddenly she was made well. Usually a person with such a **fever** would be weak

Healings LUKE 4:39-42

⁴⁰Now when the sun was setting, all those who had any that were sick with various diseases brought them to him; and he laid his hands on every one of them and healed them. ⁴¹And demons also came out of many, crying, "You are the Son of God!" But he rebuked them, and would not allow them to speak, because they knew that he was the Christ.

⁴²And when it was day he departed and went into a lonely place. And the people sought him and came to him, and would have kept him from leaving them;

---

for some time (cf. John 4:52; Acts 28:8). One can trace something of a "rebuking" theme thus far in chapter 4, even though the Greek term is used only twice. Satan was rebuked in 1-13; the Nazarenes in 16-30; the demon in 31-37; and now **the fever** (see notes 4:35). How remarkable that Jesus could control a **fever** just as he had controlled the demon. (IV)

The Sick Healed at Evening, 4:40, 41 (Matt. 8:16f.; Mark 1:32-34)

[40] The **setting sun** signaled the end of sabbath when people could travel again. The multitude, unlike Jesus, followed the interpretation which prohibited healing on sabbath and waited until sunset. His fame had spread so that people were **brought to him.** Jesus gave each individual attention. It was a personal, not a mass, healing.

[41] Note here the similarity to verses 34f., and see the notes there. Compare also Matthew 8:29; Mark 3:11f.; Acts 16:17f.; 19:15. On **Son of God,** notes 1:35; on **Christ,** notes 2:11. Note also here another instance of the "rebuking" idea seen in this chapter (see notes on vs. 39). (V)

Jesus Departs from Capernaum, 4:42-44 (Mark 1:35-39)

[42] Mark says Jesus went out "a great while before day" to pray. Luke, strangely enough, omits the reference to prayer, which may indicate the assumption his readers

LUKE 4:43—5:1 — *Synagogues of Judea*

⁴³but he said to them, "I must preach the good news of the kingdom of God to the other cities also; for I was sent for this purpose." ⁴⁴ And he was preaching in the synagogues of Judea.*

¹ While the people pressed upon him to hear the word of God, he was standing by the lake of Gennesaret.

*Other ancient authorities read *Galilee*

---

knew Mark. In numerous other cases Luke is even more interested in prayer than the other gospels (see notes on 1:10, 13). (VI)

[43] Jesus revealed that he had been **sent** with a mission (cf. 4:18, where the anointed one had been sent to proclaim; 8:1). His words formed a rebuke to those who would monopolize him and thus deny blessings to others. Here Luke uses the expression **kingdom of God** for the first time, but it recurs frequently in the gospel (see notes on 1:33). (I, VII)

[44] Apparently it became Jesus' continued custom **to teach in synagogues,** though his teaching was by no means restricted to them. One would expect Luke, at this point, to mention the ministry in Galilee, as in Mark 1:39 and Matthew 4:23-25. **Judea** means the whole country of the Jews in a number of other Lukan references (1:f; 7:17; 23:5; Acts 2:9; 10:37; 11:1; cf. Gal. 1:22), and so is not to be taken in a restricted sense here. (IV)

The Miraculous Catch of Fish, 5:1-11 (possible parallels: Matt. 4:18-22; Mark 1:16-20)

There is a symmetry in the section from 5:1 through 6:11. In the first half the call of a leading disciple (5:1-11) is followed by two healings which provoke controversy (5:12-16, 17-26). The second half begins with another call (5:27-39), followed by two sabbath controversies (6:1-11).

[1] The miracles (4:31-44) prior to this story may have been to explain why a man like Peter would unhesitatingly

Word of God   LUKE 5:1-4

² **And he saw two boats by the lake; but the fishermen had gone out of them and were washing their nets.** ³ **Getting into one of the boats, which was Simon's, he asked him to put out a little from the land. And he sat down and taught the people from the boat.** ⁴ **And when he had ceased speaking, he said to Simon, "Put out into the deep and let down your nets for a catch."**

---

respond to Jesus when the call came. With this incident a series of preaching episodes is begun, with a change from synagogue to field preaching. Jesus was experiencing increasing popularity (see 4:15, 32, 37, 40f., 42). The emphasis of the present verse is that the people **pressed upon him to hear,** not to see signs. The **lake of Gennesaret** is the Sea of Galilee.

The **word of God** in Luke refers to the kingdom proclamation (5:1 with 4:43; 8:11, 21 with 8:10; 11:28, cf. 11:20), which places a demand upon those who hear it (8:11ff., 21; 11:28). In Acts it becomes, in addition to **the word** of the kingdom (8:14 with 8:12), **the word** about Jesus. Note particularly Acts 4:31 as explained by the sermons in Acts 2:14-39 and 3:12-26. Also see Acts 6:2, 7; 11:1; 12:24; 13:5, 7, 44, 46, 48; 17:13 and 18:11. It was in Jesus, of course, that the kingdom message was fulfilled. (VI)

[2] The term for **nets** here is the most general one used to refer to **nets** of all kinds. They were cleaned of sand, pebbles, and other debris, and then hung to dry.

[3] Jesus already knew Simon (4:38f.), who may have just come from washing his nets when Jesus commandeered his boat. As on other occasions, Jesus **sat** to teach (see notes at 4:20). Separation **from land** may have been to avoid the crush of people, and to be heard and seen more easily. The boat would probably have been an open craft 20 to 30 feet long. (IV)

[4] Jesus seemed to have known of the night of fruitless fishing, but he still made what Simon thought a puzzling

LUKE 5:5-8 — *Catch of Fish*

⁵And Simon answered, "Master, we toiled all night and took nothing! But at your word I will let down the nets." ⁶And when they had done this, they enclosed a great shoal of fish; and as their nets were breaking, ⁷they beckoned to their partners in the other boat to come and help them. And they came and filled both the boats, so that they began to sink. ⁸But when Simon Peter saw it, he fell down at Jesus' knees, saying, "Depart from me, for I am a sinful man, O Lord."

---

request (cf. John 21:6). Jesus early probed the sort of faith this potential follower had.

[5] To Simon's credit, he passed the first test of faith, though his understanding of Jesus was limited (cf. John 21:3). The obedience was in spite of the fact the men had worked hard (so the Greek implies) the previous **night**. **Night** was the best fishing time, and the worst was the morning when the sun was glistening on the water. Yet **Simon** acquiesced, though his **at your word** may have been somewhat skeptical. **Master** is a word which only Luke uses in the New Testament (8:24, 45; 9:33, 49; 17:13). It implies authority of any kind with the recognition here being of Jesus' right to give orders. (VI)

[6, 7] Putting out from shore, they came to the spot where Jesus knew many **fish** could be caught. Shoals **of fish** were especially dense in Galilee. The partners' **boat** may have still been close to shore. It is interesting how Luke, with various touches (**great shoal, breaking nets,** calling **partners,** filling **both boats, began to sink**) emphasizes the greatness of this event. There are other occasions in the gospel where his skill as an artist with words is apparent.

[8] Here is another of the interesting series of reactions to Jesus traced in the stories beginning with 4:1. In the presence of the holy, **Peter** became painfully aware of his depravity. Why, then, was this experience so traumatic that **he** even **fell down** in the boat full of slithering fish? Perhaps new insight into Jesus' nature made a deep impression on

Catching Men   LUKE 5:8-12

⁹For he was astonished, and all that were with him, at the catch of fish which they had taken; ¹⁰and so also were James and John, sons of Zebedee, who were partners with Simon. And Jesus said to Simon, "Do not be afraid; henceforth you will be catching men." ¹¹And when they had brought their boats to land, they left everything and followed him.

¹²While he was in one of the cities, there came a man

---

him just at this time, especially as there was jeopardy to himself and his property. At any rate the basic concern in his mind was himself, not the marvel. (VI)

[9, 10] There may have been others present with **Simon** besides **James and John** (see other references to **James** in 6:14, 15; 8:51; 9:28, 54; 24:10; and to **John** in 6:14; 8:51; 9:28, 49, 54; 22:8). **Jesus** would not release **Simon.** But he reassured him (notes 1:12) regarding another task: **catching men.** This was the way, then, **Jesus** would respond to Simon's awareness of sin. He was not to be condemned but to be helped to usefulness. If Peter did not know what **catching men** involved, he certainly knew what **Jesus** could do. And if **catching men** were done as successfully as catching fish, it would be a signal success. (I, IV, VI)

[11] The catch, **their boats,** jobs, means of livelihood, homes, and so on, were left behind (cf. Matt. 19:27). Jesus could provide for them. Not just Peter, but the others also **followed.** Their lives came to be oriented around a new center. The discipline once devoted to fishing now was devoted to spiritual ends. There is a remarkable trust here, based on the assumption that Jesus could supply any needs as he had supplied the fish. Notice the sort of men Jesus called: they were willing to work (vs. 2), obedient to his commands (vs. 5), honest in assessing themselves (vs. 8), and willing to make whatever sacrifice his service demanded (vs. 11). (VI)

The Healing of a Leper, 5:12-16 (Matt. 8:1-4; Mark 1:40-45)

[12] Here again, Luke's stress is on the sign and the

LUKE 5:12-14 — *Leprosy*

full of leprosy; and when he saw Jesus, he fell on his face and besought him, "Lord, if you will, you can make me clean." ¹³And he stretched out his hand, and touched him, saying, "I will; be clean." And immediately the leprosy left him. ¹⁴And he charged him to tell no one; but "go and show yourself to the priest, and make an offering for your cleansing, as Moses commanded, for a proof to the people."*

*Greek *to them*

---

reaction, rather than on the person being healed. The Greek term for **leprosy** was general, and included several skin diseases, so that it is impossible to know the exact nature of the man's affliction. Perhaps Luke meant to indicate it was of a severe sort by **full of**. On the healing of lepers see Numbers 12:13; Matthew 10:8; 11:5; and Luke 17:12. Leviticus 13:1-59 describes the provisions of the law for the diseases generally called **leprosy** (the Hebrew word had the same vagueness as the Greek), and the next chapter prescribes the rituals for cleansing. Whatever the nature of the case, Jesus had compassion on the pathetic **man.** (VI)

Besought, sometimes translated "pray," is found elsewhere in Luke at 8:28, 38; 9:38, 40; 10:2; 21:36 and 22:32. Just over half the total New Testament usages of this word are in the Lukan writings. See discussion at 1:10.

[13] It would appear unusual for Jesus to touch such a man. He could have healed him without it, but the touch showed clearly his mastery over the disease and compassion for the man.

[14] The word for **charged** is from a verb sometimes used of commanders whose orders were passed along the line (see 17:14). The puzzle is why Jesus forbade the man **to tell.** Various suggestions have been offered. Perhaps the law was to be obeyed before the man did anything else (Mark says that Jesus sternly charged him and sent him away at once), or the man was to be kept from too much

Jesus' Popularity   LUKE 5:14-17

¹⁵But so much the more the report went abroad concerning him; and great multitudes gathered to hear and to be healed of their infirmities. ¹⁶But he withdrew to the wilderness and prayed.
¹⁷On one of those days, as he was teaching, there were Pharisees and teachers of the law sitting by, who had come from every village of Galilee and Judea and from Jerusalem;

---

pride in boasting of his healing, or there was an intent to prevent too much unnecessary excitement among the people (this is the implication of Mark 1:45).

The ritual of **cleansing** was to follow the procedure outlined in Leviticus 14:1-32. Nothing was said there, however, about a proof. Probably Jesus knew the people would inevitably hear of the healing, so he wanted them also to know of his respect for the law. (IV, V)

[15] Mark notes that Jesus could not enter a town for the press of people and implies that even in the country he was not always left alone. This was because (as Mark notes) the leper disobeyed and spread the news about (cf. 4:14, 37). (V, VI)

[16] Mark has the withdrawal for prayer before the healing of the leper (1:35). Some see this verse referring to Jesus' practice on this particular occasion, whereas other translators indicate it was a thing he did customarily. Both could quite easily be true. The text likely means the multitudes were coming, but he was engaging in prayer (and was thus inaccessible). Jesus established priorities in his life, and though preaching and healing were of great importance, at times prayer and retirement were even more important (see notes at 1:10).

The Healing of the Paralytic, 5:17-26 (Matt. 9:1-8; Mark 2:1-12)

[17] This story forms a climax of the miracle series, stretching back to 4:31. Forgiving sins was the greatest of

LUKE 5:17-20 — *Conflict Stories*

and the power of the Lord was with him to heal.*[p]* [18] And behold, men were bringing on a bed a man who was paralyzed, and they sought to bring him in and lay him before Jesus;*[q]* [19] but finding no way to bring him in, because of the crowd, they went up on the roof and let him down with his bed through the tiles into the midst before Jesus. [20] And when he saw their faith he said, "Man, your sins are forgiven you."

> [p] Other ancient authorities read *was present to heal them*
> [q] Greek *him*

---

his mighty deeds. In this episode and the incidents through 6:11, **the law** or religious tradition of the Jews is involved. This is also the first of five incidents (all paralleled in Mark) which showed the authority of Jesus. Whereas the preceding stories from 4:13 have shown Jesus' popularity (but cf. 4:28f.), in these five stories the accounts concern conflict.

Mark locates this event in Capernaum. Only Luke notes that **Pharisees and teachers** were present. In rabbinic writings **teachers** were those who gave authoritative interpretations of scripture. Josephus says the **Pharisees** had six thousand members at this time, and they were admired by practically all the Jews. People were there **from Galilee and Judea,** showing something of the spread of Jesus' reputation. On **Jerusalem,** see notes at 2:22; on **power,** see notes at 1:17. (IV)

[18, 19] These verses indicate to what lengths people would go to get to **Jesus.** It was ironic that so many people wanted to see **Jesus** that they prevented the **paralytic** (at first) from getting to him. (VI)

[20] If there were a popular belief that sin caused illness, then a man could never know he was **forgiven** till he was cured. Yet it is not at all certain that this was the prevailing opinion. Jesus may have known that sin was at the root of the man's paralysis, or the cause of the illness may have been irrelevant. The affirmation of the connection may have

Faith and Forgiveness LUKE 5:20-23

²¹ And the scribes and the Pharisees began to question, saying, "Who is this that speaks blasphemies? Who can forgive sins but God only?" ²² When Jesus perceived their questionings, he answered them, "Why do you question in your hearts? ²³ Which is easier, to say, 'Your sins are forgiven you,' or to say, 'Rise and walk'?

---

been only generic, i.e., Jesus was simply saying that he came to do more than just heal the body. In any event, Jesus' response was strange and unexpected. He certainly knew his words would occasion thought and comment. And here Luke gives an important element in his depiction of Jesus (see notes at 1:77; 3:3). Jesus knew that men of **faith** would be willing at least to consider accepting him as sin-forgiver as well as healer (see 7:48). For other uses of the word **faith** see 7:9, 50; 8:25, 48; 17:5, 6, 19; 18:8, 42; 22:32. (I)

[21] The **scribes** were professional lawyers, whose chief business was teaching and interpreting the law. The first question in Mark's account asked, "Why does this man speak thus?" But Luke, whose telling of the incident focuses more on the identity of Jesus, has the question **Who?** The second question was not asked amiss, but the questioners were not willing to accept all evidence leading to an answer (see 7:49). (IV, VI)

[22] They seem not to have spoken their doubts directly to **Jesus,** or so the word for **questionings** ("thoughts" rather than "discussions") seems to imply. But **Jesus** knew what they thought. The word **perceived** even indicates thorough and accurate knowledge. (III, VI)

[23] Speech is cheap, but deeds are weighty. If Jesus could do the visible, at least the presumption would be his power to do the invisible. Not that every wonder worker could forgive **sins,** but who would know his own power better than the one possessing it? At the least, a miracle

LUKE 5:23, 24 *Son of Man*

²⁴"But that you may know that the Son of man has authority on earth to forgive sins" — he said to the man who was paralyzed — "I say to you, rise, take up your bed, and go home."

---

would demand that they give careful attention to Jesus' claim to forgive (cf. John 5:36).

[24] This is the first case in which Luke mentions the frequently used title, **Son of man** (other references are 6:5, 22; 7:34; 9:22, 26, 44, 58; 11:30; 12:8, 10, 40; 17:22, 24, 26, 30; 18:8, 31; 19:10; 21:27, 36; 22:22, 48, 69; 24:7). Several suggestions have been made regarding the background of the term. In the Old Testament it was used frequently to refer to Ezekiel (2:1 and ninety-two other times). It was also found in the sense "human being" in the Psalms (8:4; 80:17; 144:3; 146:3). The intertestamental *Book of Enoch* used the term of a supernatural figure. But the most likely background of Jesus' usage was the figure of Daniel 7:13f. who ascended to the Ancient of Days and received a kingdom.

It is also possible that upon some occasions the term was meant to refer to Jesus as a typical human being. The problem is that Jesus did not always make his meaning clear, although some passages yield distinct meanings. Perhaps Jesus deliberately chose a term of some ambiguity so he could mold it into the significance he wished. As a messianic term it may have been freer of political overtones than many he could use.

If one examines the references in Luke, a picture of **the Son of man** emerges which involves the following elements. He was an authoritative figure who had power **to forgive sins** (5:24) and was lord of the sabbath (6:5). He was a sign to his generation (11:30). He came to seek and save the lost (19:10). He would suffer, be killed, and be raised the third day (9:22 and often), and his followers would also suffer (6:22). Having been raised, he would sit at the right hand of the Father (22:69), from whence he would

Levi   LUKE 5:24-28

[25] And immediately he rose before them, and took up that on which he lay, and went home, glorifying God. [26] And amazement seized them all, and they glorified God and were filled with awe, saying, "We have seen strange things today."

[27] After this he went out, and saw a tax collector, named Levi, sitting at the tax office; and he said to him, "Follow me." [28] And he left everything, and rose and followed him.

---

one day return as a judge (9:26; 12:8). (IV) Jesus frequently called himself **the Son of man**, but the description is never used of him in the gospels by another (but see Acts 7:56; Rev. 1:13; 14:14). (II) On **authority,** see notes at 4:32.

[25, 26] No time was wasted in effecting the wonder (see John 5:8f.). Luke, characteristically, stresses reactions. The people were **all** amazed (including the critics?), but whether they believed in Jesus is not indicated. The healed man would have **glorified God** both for healing and for forgiveness. With the impressive reaction recorded in verse 26, this sequence of miracles (4:31 — 5:26) comes to an end. On fear, see notes at 1:12; on glorify, see notes at 2:20. (VI)

The Call of Levi, 5:27-32 (Matt. 9:9-13; Mark 2:13-17)

[27] Here is a second consecutive story in which Jesus challenged the orthodox thinking of his day. **Levi** was called Matthew in the first gospel. Mark identifies him as the son of Alphaeus. It was strange that Jesus would call him, but the Lord saw something in this **tax collector** (see notes at 3:12f.). Calling of such a man was a part of the new teaching that would not fit old patterns (vss. 36f.). There is no indication Jesus had met him before, but the circumstances of this passage can be more easily understood had there been prior acquaintance. Yet it is not totally impossible a man would leave all for Jesus, even on first meeting. (III, IV)

[28] Only Luke says that Levi **left** all to follow. (VI, VIII)

LUKE 5:29, 30 — *Levi's Dinner*

²⁹ And Levi made him a great feast in his house; and there was a large company of tax collectors and others sitting at table ʳ with them. ³⁰ And the Pharisees and their scribes murmured against his disciples, saying, "Why do you eat and drink with tax collectors and sinners?"

ʳ Greek *reclining*

---

[29] Only Luke is so explicit in indicating the meal was at Levi's home. If **Levi** resigned his post, this could have been a farewell dinner for his colleagues. It was a strange meal, with the one who claimed to forgive men in association with all the "wrong" people (Matthew and Mark say "sinners"). (VI) This is the first of a number of cases in Luke that involve a meal. Others are 5:33-35; 7:34, 36-50; 9:12-17; 10:7, 38-42; 11:37ff.; 12:35-38, 41-43; 13:24, 26, 29f.; 14:1, 7-11, 12-14, 15-24; 15:2, 22-30; 22:7-23, 29, 30; 24:30-32, 41-43.

[30] For the first time in Luke, the **disciples** of Jesus are mentioned as such. Whereas in Matthew and Mark Jesus was criticized directly, in Luke the critics came to his followers (see 15:1, 19:7; cf. also 7:34). It is almost as if **the Pharisees** were trying to demonstrate to them why a man like Jesus wasn't worth following.

The **scribes** of **the Pharisees** were so called to distinguish them from **scribes** of other Jewish parties (see notes at 5:21). Though **the Pharisees** doubted Jesus could forgive sin, this is their first hostile action recorded by Luke. These critics probably were not invited, nor would they have come if they had been. The Mishnah (*Berakoth* 43) expressly states the disciples of the **scribes** could have no table communion with such people. It is not known exactly when this tradition began, but it likely was in effect at the time of Jesus. Since uninvited guests would often stand around the edge of an Oriental feast, the critics may have been there in such a role. Their criticism implied that no righteous man would associate with such people as did Jesus. In their concern for rules, **the Pharisees and scribes** neglected a more

Righteous and Sinners   LUKE 5:30-33

[31] And Jesus answered them, "Those who are well have no need of a physician, but those who are sick; [32] I have not come to call the righteous, but sinners to repentance."

[33] And they said to him, "The disciples of John fast often and offer prayers, and so do the disciples of the Pharisees, but yours eat and drink."

---

important concern, one which Jesus emphasized—concern for people. (VI)

[31, 32] This is an important statement regarding Jesus' mission, as was 4:43. The **call,** in light of the meal context, may have implied the idea of an invitation to the messianic feast. The expression **to repentance** is not found in the parallels, and is in accord with Luke's emphasis (see notes at 3:3).

Jesus accepted responsibility for the people at the meal, relieving Levi of blame. It may have been that some of the specific guests had been asked at his suggestion. It was obvious that those invited were **sinners.** In addition, **Jesus** may have meant that **the righteous** (see notes at 1:6) were the self-righteous who, if they would recognize it, were greater **sinners** than those at the feast. If they would see their need, **Jesus** would help them, too. He may also have been saying to the critics, "If you are spiritual physicians, why aren't you helping these, who are obviously **sick,** instead of avoiding them?" Jewish scholars point out that one new thing **Jesus** brought to the Judaism of his day was a seeking for **sinners** rather than shunning them. (I, IV)

The Question About Fasting, 5:33-39 (Matt 9:14-17; Mark 2:18-22)

[33] Here is a third controversy centered in Jewish religious tradition. If Jesus were religious why didn't he keep the traditions religious people kept? If this dialogue did not come in the context of the meal at Levi's house, then Luke probably included it here because it fit the theme of the context.

LUKE 5:33-36 — *Fasting*

³⁴ And Jesus said to them, "Can you make wedding guests fast while the bridegroom is with them? ³⁵ The days will come, when the bridegroom is taken away from them, and then they will fast in those days." ³⁶ He told them a parable also: "No one tears a piece from a new garment and puts it upon an old garment; if he does, he will tear the new, and the piece from the new will not match the old.

Only Luke mentions the prayer of John's and Jesus' **disciples.** One would expect him to do so (notes at 1:13), though in the further discussion the prayer idea drops out. Perhaps Jesus' **disciples** did not keep the fixed ritual of times of prayer that characterized pious Jews. Yet they would be instructed by Jesus regarding new dimensions of prayer (11:1-4).

The fasts may have been the regular Monday and Thursday fasts of the Jews (Luke 18:12; *Didache* 8:1). These were traditional, since the only fasts of universal obligation enjoined by the law were in connection with the Day of Atonement (Lev. 16; 23:26-32). On other fasts compare Zechariah 7:5; 8:19. Jesus did practice fasting upon occasion (4:2) and allowed it as a voluntary spiritual discipline, but he did not make it a compulsory ordinance. On meals, see notes at 5:29. (VI)

[34, 35] A **wedding** would be an exception even to the regular rule for fasting. So fasting could be superseded, as **Jesus** suggested was the case regarding his presence. His coming was a joyous, not a somber, occasion. (IV)

The reference to future fasting of the disciples might be an intimation of Jesus' coming death and departure (cf. 17:22). If so, it is the first such indication in the gospel, but was appropriate in connection with the record of the first open opposition from Jewish leaders (see notes at 9:22). (IV)

[36] Luke's record points out the damage done to both

New and Old LUKE 5:36-38

³⁷ **And no one puts new wine into old wineskins; if he does, the new wine will burst the skins and it will be spilled, and the skins will be destroyed. ³⁸ But new wine must be put into fresh wineskins.**

---

the **new** (torn) and **old** (not matched) if such a patching job were done. The problem is that Jesus did not explain these sayings, and in explaining them the modern reader must not try to read too much into the text. However, they obviously have to do with imposing the old customs of fasting and prayer upon the new teaching Jesus brought. Whether **the old** refers to the ways of the Pharisees or to those of John's disciples, Jesus brought something **new**. It may have likenesses to, and in part be built upon, **the old.** Yet it must be judged by its own standards. To bind Jewish prayer and fasting customs on Jesus' disciples would deny the system for which they were being trained. Thus, by this and the next saying, Jesus indicated something of his authority and of the fact he was inaugurating a new state in man's relation to God.

[37, 38] This saying carries on the idea of the first. Here the **wine** represented all the **new** custom, whereas the cloth was just a fragment of it. Also the garments were only marred, while **the skins** were destroyed and **the wine** lost (cf. Job 32:19). Finally, Jesus here not only condemned the method but gave the right one.

Wineskins were made from a single goatskin from which the flesh and bone were drawn without ripping the skin. The neck of the goat became the neck of the "bottle." The skin was soft and pliable and could expand with the fermenting **new wine.** But an **old** skin became brittle and would not expand. It would burst, if subjected to the strain of fermentation.

So the point seems to be that a **new** and growing system could not be forced into the forms of an **old** one. The strong **new** life principle would shatter the **old** forms (as indeed

LUKE 5:38—6:1   *Old Wine*

³⁹ And no one after drinking old wine desires new; for he says, 'The old is good.' "*

¹ On a sabbath,' while he was going through the grainfields, his disciples plucked and ate some ears of grain, rubbing them in their hands.

<small>*Other ancient authorities read *better*
' Other ancient authorities read *On the second first sabbath* (on the second sabbath after the first)</small>

---

the presence of Jesus seemed to be doing in the verses from 5:17 to present).

[39] This saying is unique to Luke. The point is not the relative merit of the wines, as some might infer from comparison with verses 37f. Rather the depiction is of "pious conservatism." To them the right was **the old.** This explained why the Pharisees and other critics of Jesus would not stand for his activities and his message and why they were unwilling to countenance any change.

These sayings, coming after a series of controversies and before two others (6:1-11), indicate that Jesus had a **new** thing to offer and that he was to encounter opposition from those to whom **the old** was **good.** The gospel develops this conflict dramatically till it ultimately led to the cross.

Plucking Ears of Grain on the Sabbath, 6:1-5 (Matt. 12:1-8; Mark 2:23-28)

[1] Jesus' challenge to the traditional Jewish religious conceptions of his day this time concerned the **sabbath** and what was lawful (verses 2, 4, 9). Jesus' **disciples** may have been with him on a preaching tour and apparently were very hungry. Thus, their mission took precedence over the Jewish ritual. Exodus 20:8-11 forbade work on the **sabbath.** The Jews had elaborated the **sabbath** requirements to define precisely what was work, and had arranged their strictures in thirty-nine categories. According to those elaborations, the **disciples** were guilty of reaping, threshing, winnowing, and preparing a meal. They probably did not violate the

Sabbath Observance LUKE 6:1-5

²But some of the Pharisees said, "Why are you doing what is not lawful to do on the sabbath?" ³And Jesus answered, "Have you not read what David did when he was hungry, he and those who were with him: ⁴how he entered the house of God, and took and ate the bread of the Presence, which it is not lawful for any but the priests to eat, and also gave it to those with him?" ⁵And he said to them, "The Son of man is lord of the sabbath."

---

limits of **a sabbath** journey, since that was not mentioned. Deuteronomy 23:25 allowed taking grain from a field, so their wrong was not theft. The **ears of grain** were probably the heads of the stalks, and the **rubbing** would be to get rid of the chaff.

[2] Luke, in contrast to Matthew and Mark, has Jesus included in the criticism of **the Pharisees. (VI)**

[3, 4] The priest gave David **the bread,** thereby investing the act with his authority (1 Sam. 21:1-7). The Jews felt the sabbath rules could be suspended when life was in danger (*Shabbath* 132a; *Yoma* 8:6) and that David's case was similar to such exceptions, though not involving the sabbath. The law of **the bread,** in Leviticus 24:5-9, though specifying the food was to be eaten by Aaron and his descendants in a holy place, did not specifically prohibit others from eating. In emergency it was recognized as permissible to go beyond the law, on the principle that human need transcended the ceremonial requirement. Since **the bread** was to provide, in part, for human (i.e., the priest's) need, it would be a violation of the spirit of the law to refuse **David** and thus augment, rather than alleviate, need. Jesus did not think the letter of the law was insignificant, but he did not want the spirit to be violated by a meticulous insistence on the letter.

[5] Jesus' dominant defense here was an assertion of his authority. Jesus, because of what he was, had the right to act as he did (see John 5:17). This is shown further by the

LUKE 6:5-9 *Lord of the Sabbath*

⁶On another sabbath, when he entered the synagogue and taught, a man was there whose right hand was withered. ⁷And the scribes and the Pharisees watched him, to see whether he would heal on the sabbath, so that they might find an accusation against him. ⁸But he knew their thoughts, and he said to the man who had the withered hand, "Come and stand here." And he rose and stood there. ⁹And Jesus said to them, "I ask you, is it lawful on the sabbath to do good or to do harm, to save life or to destroy it?"

---

fact that **lord** comes first in the Greek phrase, thus emphasizing it. Jesus, in claiming leadership over **the sabbath**, would thus be indirectly asserting the messianic age had come. Note his authority over the law of Moses here, as over sin in 5:24. On **Son of man,** see notes 5:24. (IV)

The Healing of the Man with the Withered Hand, 6:6-11 (Matt. 12:9-14; Mark 3:1-6)

[6, 7] Jesus entered **the synagogue** primarily to teach. Only Luke notes that it was the man's **right hand** that **was withered.** This event was on a later day than the preceding, though Matthew and Mark might indicate, on cursory reading, that the two were on the same day.

The man did not request healing. It was almost as if Jesus deliberately baited his critics so he could make his point. The purpose of the miracle was to make Jesus' point about compassion and **the sabbath.** The critics, perhaps assuming Jesus healed any sick around him, **watched** (the verb implies watching with sinister intent) to find if he would violate **sabbath** tradition (cf. 14:1; 20:20). (VI)

[8] Jesus had the disconcerting ability to know what others thought (III; see also Matt. 9:4; 12:25; John 2:25). The man was told to **stand,** and one can imagine Jesus' critics becoming alert. He made no secret of what he intended to do, being as open as they were covert.

[9] Suddenly the scribes and Pharisees found themselves

Sabbath Healing LUKE 6:9-11

¹⁰ And he looked around on them all, and said to him, "Stretch out your hand." And he did so, and his hand was restored. ¹¹ But they were filled with fury and discussed with one another what they might do to Jesus.

---

the quarry instead of the hunters. As Jesus had been asked, "Is it lawful?" (vs. 2), so he turned the question on his would-be critics. They knew that a number of "dangerous" diseases could be healed **on the sabbath** without violation of custom. If **life** could be saved, could not **good** as logically be done? How could they deny Jesus this right when they were doing the harm of watching Jesus with evil intent **on the sabbath**? Had not Jesus more right to **do good** than they to **do harm**? Save is found in Luke also at 7:50; 8:12, 36, 48, 50; 9:24, 56; 13:23; 17:19; 18:26, 42; 19:10; 23:35, 37, 39.

[10, 11] Jesus **looked** at the people (Mark notes "with anger"), who did not answer his question, perhaps because they saw they were trapped. The man was not given a healing touch but told to extend his **hand**. Strictly speaking, the words were not a healing formula, so that any accusation against Jesus had to be based on implications concerning his power.

The critics were insensitive to the marvelous deed and the joy of the healed man. Instead they reacted **with fury**, thus doing harm on the sabbath (see especially Matthew and Mark). It could have been caused by their zeal for the sabbath but was more likely frustration because Jesus had so neatly countered their unspoken criticisms. They began to plot how to handle him, so the pattern of rejection which Luke so skillfully depicts here moves to even greater intensity than before. (IV, VI)

THE MIDDLE MINISTRY, 6:12—8:56

The present section stresses more fully the ideas found in 4:14-6:11. The heart of Jesus' teaching is at last given

LUKE 6:12, 13

> [12] In these days he went out into the hills to pray; and all night he continued in prayer to God. [13] And when it was day, he called his disciples, and chose from them twelve, whom he named apostles;

(6:20-49). Following this are two miracles and the teaching about John. The latter may well be the key to the section, since the messianic signs described there (7:22f.; see 4:18f.) are found also in his preaching (6:20-49, note especially the initial mention of the poor; 8:5-21, with stress on how people hear), healings (7:1-10, 11-17; 8:26-39, 40-56), and a nature miracle (8:22-25). Reactions to Jesus are featured prominently (especially 7:16, 19, 49; 8:25, 37f., 47, 56). The section shows the universality of Jesus' concerns (a Gentile, 7:1-10; a sinful woman, 7:36-50), and his compassion (7:13).

All of these things are set against the background of the choice of the twelve (6:12-16). In both teaching sections (6:20-49 and 8:5-21) miracle stories follow immediately, and in both cases four stories follow the teaching section before the beginning of the next section. Also in both sections following the miracle stories there is a story stressing the importance of faith (7:50; 8:48).

The Call of the Twelve, 6:12-16 (Matt. 10:1-4; Mark 3:13-19)

[12] In the remainder of chapter six and in chapter seven Luke stresses the character and the recipients of the coming age. This **all night prayer** preceding the choice of the twelve and the sermon on the plain is mentioned only by Luke (but cf. Matt. 14:23). On prayer, see notes at 1:10. (IV)

[13] These **twelve** might be seen as corresponding to the **twelve** tribe framework of the first Israel (cf. 22:30) and in a sense as the foundation of the new Israel. Luke makes their selection from a larger group of **disciples** more explicit than Matthew and Mark. This chosen group was to have special tasks and authority from Jesus and would find themselves even more tightly knit to him than his other followers. They were a diverse group, including such men as a tax

Twelve Apostles   LUKE 6:13-18

[14] Simon, whom he named **Peter**, and **Andrew** his brother, and **James** and **John**, and **Philip** and **Bartholomew**, [15] and **Matthew**, and **Thomas**, and **James the son of Alphaeus**, and **Simon who was called the Zealot**, [16] and **Judas the son of James**, and **Judas Iscariot**, who became a traitor.

[17] And he came down with them and stood on a level place, with a great crowd of his disciples and a great multitude

---

collector and a Zealot, incorporated in the same close fellowship.

[14-16] **Simon** comes first in all three gospel lists, as **Judas** comes last in all. All are arranged in three groups, with the same four names in the first group. From this point Luke uses the name **Peter** instead of **Simon** (22:31 and 24:34 are quotations from others). Prior to this he was never called just **Peter**. It was a custom of Jewish rabbis to give their disciples surnames (*Pirke Aboth* 2:10).

Only John gives information about **Andrew** (1:40, 44; 6:8f.; 12:22), **Philip** (6:5, 7; 12:21f.; 14:8f.), and **Thomas** (11:16; 14:5; 20:24-29). **James of Alphaeus** probably was the same as **James** the less of Matthew 27:56 and Mark 15:40. **Simon** was also called the Canaanaean, which was the Aramaic equivalent for **Zealot** (not a place name). **Zealot** probably indicated one with a particular zeal for the law who may have entertained avid nationalistic views. Actually, it is impossible to know if the term was meant in a religious or patriotic sense here. He was probably so designated to distinguish him from **Simon Peter**. **Judas of James** (perhaps his brother, but more likely son) was probably the same as Thaddaeus of Matthew and Mark. **Iscariot**, in reference to the other **Judas**, is a term of uncertain meaning, with one of several logical explanations being that it was a place name.

Jesus Heals the Multitudes, 6:17-19 (possible parallels, Matt. 12:15-21; Mark 3:7-12; see also Matt. 4:23-5:1)

[17, 18] Here the **people** were waiting for him as he

LUKE 6:17-20 — *Healings*

of people from all Judea and Jerusalem and the seacoast of Tyre and Sidon, who came to hear him and to be healed of their diseases; [18] and those who were troubled with unclean spirits were cured. [19] And all the crowd sought to touch him, for power came forth from him and healed them all.

[20] And he lifted up his eyes on his disciples, and said:
"Blessed are you poor, for yours is the kingdom of God.

---

descended the mountain (on multitudes, see notes at 1:10). The group was from an interesting variety of locales. Luke has not previously mentioned **Tyre and Sidon**. Perhaps Gentiles were in the number. Likely not all of those present were **disciples** of Jesus, though it was to his followers (real and prospective) that he addressed himself (vs. 20). Again the twofold nature of Jesus' ministry, teaching and healing, is indicated. (VI)

[19] It is doubtful that there was a special quality to contact with Jesus. Rather, he no doubt exercised his will to heal as he was touched (see Mark 5:27-30). On **power**, see notes at 1:17. (IV, VI)

The Sermon on the Plain: The Beatitudes, 6:20-23 (Matt. 5:3, 4, 6, 11, 12)

[20] Though this passage (20-49) may be identified with the Sermon on the Mount (Matt. 5-7), it is possible that Jesus delivered similar teachings on different occasions, or that both Matthew and Luke used the occasions of these great sermons to present a complex of the teachings of the Lord in a way consonant with the purposes of their respective gospels. Forty-one verses from the Sermon on the Mount are not paralleled in Luke. Yet the plan of both is the same, with a general movement from qualities of disciples, to their duties, to the idea of judgment. In Matthew Jesus' words are given in the third person, whereas Luke's use of the second person depicts Jesus as addressing his audience personally.

This sermon embodies the substance of the message

Jesus' Teaching LUKE 6:20-22

²¹ "Blessed are you that hunger now, for you shall be satisfied.

"Blessed are you that weep now, for you shall laugh.

²² "Blessed are you when men hate you, and when they exclude you and revile you, and cast out your name as evil, on account of the Son of man!

Jesus had been teaching. The blessedness of the **poor** was a messianic sign (4:17f.; 7:22f.). But who were they? Some would argue the meaning is basically the same as Matthew's "poor in spirit." Yet a study of Luke's concept of the **poor** (see notes at 4:18f.; cf. 1:53; 6:24; VI) would indicate he has the literally **poor** in mind. In the centuries before Christ the Jews saw the **poor** as the saintly or pious (Isa. 66:1f.; cf. James 2:5). Perhaps the reference was to those who went, in that society, without human justice. Parallels in the Dead Sea Scrolls indicate **poor** may describe those who counted worldly goods as nothing and accepted voluntary want. But if men adopted such a life for the sake of the Lord, this would be more than compensated by their possession of the **kingdom of God** (cf. Isa. 57:15; notes at 1:33). (I)

[21] Though Matthew 5:6 specifies those hungering and thirsting for righteousness, we see these as literally hungry, and for the reasons expressed above (vs. 20). The satisfaction likely refers to the spiritual satisfaction that would compensate those willing to accept **hunger** for God's sake (parallel to the kingdom of God). (VIII)

The second beatitude in verse 21, though similar to Matthew 5:4, is unique in its particular expression. One can assume the weeping to be literal and that the interpretation should be the same, necessary changes being made, as in the two previous beatitudes. Men who weep because of their service to God, or because of the world's refusal to serve him, or because of their own sorrow or want, or because of persecution, come to experience joy (cf. Ps. 126:5f.; see notes at 1:14, 47, 58f.).

[22] Though all the beatitudes involve a paradox, here

LUKE 6:22-25 — *Spiritual Happiness*

²³ Rejoice in that day, and leap for joy, for behold, your reward is great in heaven; for so their fathers did to the prophets.

²⁴ "But woe to you that are rich, for you have received your consolation.

²⁵ "Woe to you that are full now, for you shall hunger.

---

it is more evident than in the preceding three. One would not expect a poor, hungry, weeping, or persecuted man to be **blessed**, or happy. Yet Jesus reverses normal expectations by speaking of a higher plane of activity. These people, dissatisfied and rejected by the present age, are yet the greater beneficiaries of God's bounty.

[23] Those who are hated will enjoy both God's **reward** and the assurance of fellowship with saintly company. On **rejoice**, see notes at 1:14. There was no promise that suffering would be removed, but it would be ultimately forgotten in the reception of great blessing. Suffering, regardless of the evaluation of those who view it superficially, can be borne joyfully when the mind is transformed by attention to greater goals and values (cf. Rom. 5:1-5). (I, VII)

The Sermon on the Plain; The Woes, 6:24-26

[24] These woes, which reverse the blessings, find no parallel in Matthew. **Woe** (*ouai*) expressed lamentation, not denunciation (see James 5:1). Yet riches, being **full**, laughing, and being spoken well of were certainly not wrong in themselves. Thus, one must assume some other conditions implied in Jesus' words. Perhaps these people were the persecutors of those in the kingdom. But more probably they were those to whom these things were more important than the relation they sustained to the Lord. A man must choose his reward. It either can be of this age (vss. 24-26) or of the age to come (vss. 20-23). Compare Matthew 6:1-17.

The noun for **rich** is found also in Luke at 12:16; 14:12; 16:1, 19, 21, 22; 18:23, 25; 19:2; 21:1; see the verb at 1:53.

[25] The **full**, i.e., those satisfied with nothing more than

Woes   LUKE 6:25-28

"Woe to you that laugh now, for you shall mourn and weep.

[26] "Woe to you, when all men speak well of you, for so their fathers did to the false prophets.

[27] "But I say to you that hear, Love your enemies, do good to those who hate you, [28] bless those who curse you, pray for those who abuse you.

---

physical fulness, would eventually know a starvation of spiritual food. These could be individuals impervious to the needs of those around them (cf. 12:19f.; 16:25; James 5:1-5). (VIII)

Those that laughed but were indifferent to things of the kingdom would discover they had missed the real source of joy and would experience mourning and weeping (cf. James 4:9; on joy see notes at 1:14, 47, 58). (VII)

[26] Since being well-spoken of was not wrong in itself, Jesus may have meant those who curried favor at any cost and who would achieve their immediate goal but who were no more God's people than **the false prophets** (see Micah 2:11). In some cases men who were well spoken of by all would be so only because they had compromised the kingdom (see James 4:4).

The Sermon on the Plain: On Love of One's Enemies, 6:27-36 (Matt. 5:39-42, 44-48; 7:12)

[27, 28] Matthew 5:44 is similar to these verses. However, in this paragraph Luke combines sayings from the last two contrasts in Matthew 5 (38-42, 43-48), plus the golden rule (Matt. 7:12). In the present verses the second and third statements (**bless . . . pray . . .**) are not found in Matthew. The behavior in these verses is active, while that indicated in 29f. is more responsive.

Luke orients the discussion in terms of **love** more than Matthew. One distinctive thing about Christian **love** was **love** for one's **enemies**. Here for the first time this gospel

LUKE 6:27-30 — *Love of Enemies*

²⁹ To him who strikes you on the cheek, offer the other also; and from him who takes away your cloak do not withhold your coat as well. ³⁰ Give to every one who begs from you; and of him who takes away your goods do not ask them again.

---

uses the verb *agapaō*, which describes a non-selective **love** based in the very nature of God himself. It is not bestowed because of the loveableness of the object loved but because of the loving nature of the one who bestows it (see Matt. 5:43-48; also Luke 14:12-16). Other Lukan usages of this verb are 6:32, 35; 7:5, 42, 47; 10:27; 11:43; 16:13. This **love** becomes the central point of Christian ethics (see Rom. 12:17; 13:8-10). One who adopts it becomes not simply obedient to moral admonitions but is transformed into the very nature of God. It is natural to **love** "loved ones," but it takes an act of a transformed will to **love** an enemy. In a society where Roman power was hated, and where kingdom expectations would be seen in such a political context, words like this from a Messiah were remarkable indeed.

Further amplification of this imperative involved doing **good to those** hating one, blessing those cursing one, and praying for one's abusers (see notes at 1:10). Jesus would demonstrate these in a remarkable way in his life (23:34).

[29] Here is further explication of the love ethic. Matthew 5:39f. sets the sayings in a legal context and in the discussion of retaliation. The **cloak** was the outer and costlier garment, more likely to be taken, while the **coat** was the under. Jesus taught that retaliation or protection of material possessions is less important than loving, human relations. Though it would be hard to love the person inflicting the harm, it was this that made the teaching of Jesus different.

[30] The parallel to this verse is Matthew 5:42, where the saying is placed in the paragraph on love. Jesus was not speaking about perfunctory offerings to the poor but of a moral concern which expressed itself in self-denial for the sake of others. Love gives for the sake of giving, not

The Love Ethic   **LUKE 6:30-34**

[31] And as you wish that men would do to you, do so to them.

[32] "If you love those who love you, what credit is that to you? For even sinners love those who love them. [33] And if you do good to those who do good to you, what credit is that to you? For even sinners do the same. [34] And if you lend to those from whom you hope to receive, what credit is that to you? Even sinners lend to sinners, to receive as much again.

---

for the sake of return. When one must choose between goods and persons, persons are more important. Yet one might choose to refuse a gift of money to a professional beggar if he might use it to his harm and be acting in greater love than if he gave the gift (see 2 Thess. 3:10-12). Jesus was not thinking of those who took advantage of others in their self-destructive lethargy but rather of the genuinely needy. (VIII)

[31] The parallel is in Matthew 7:12. The golden rule is meaningful against the background of the love ethic. Otherwise a masochist could punish others to be punished in return.

Jesus was apparently the first to express this idea in positive form, though a negative form can be documented earlier, as, e.g., in the teachings of Hillel ("What is hateful to you do not to your neighbor: that is the whole Torah, while the rest is commentary," *Sanhedrin* 31a).

[32, 33] There is a natural love (see notes at 6:27) which is innate and therefore not virtuous in the special sense of the kingdom ethic (but cf. 1 Tim. 5:8). Virtue is what one develops beyond nature. Disciples were to be more than the sinners were.

[34] There is no parallel to this saying in Matthew (but see Lev. 25:35-38). The lending here was that done upon interest. Jesus was no more condemning lending at interest than he condemned natural love in the preceding verse. He was speaking about ethical human relations. One is to act when there is no benefit to be gained from the other. Love

LUKE 6:34-37 — *Do Good to All*

[35] But love your enemies, and do good, and lend, expecting nothing in return;[*] and your reward will be great, and you will be sons of the Most High; for he is kind to the ungrateful and the selfish. [36] Be merciful, even as your Father is merciful.

[37] "Judge not, and you will not be judged; condemn not, and you will not be condemned; forgive, and you will be forgiven;

[*] Other ancient authorities read *despairing of no man*

---

is given for the benefit it can bestow upon the beloved, not for selfish gain. In fact, love cannot possibly be bestowed for material gain. (VIII)

[35] Jesus returns to the statement of verse 27, now adding a discussion of the real benefits and rationale that lead one to such loving action. **Expecting nothing in return** has an alternate reading, "despairing of no man," which would indicate the need of patience even when the most negative response was elicited by one's good deeds. The passage, as it reads, might imply that a loan was to be made even if the principal were not returned and, if so, advances from the idea of verse 34. The **reward** (cf. Matt. 6:1, 2, 4, etc.) would come both in service and subsequent to it. The rationale for loving action is the nature of God, who blesses all men impartially. To be loving makes one a partaker in God's nature (i.e., a son **of the Most High**). Jesus repudiated the doctrine that God punishes the wicked in this life by specific withholding of nature's blessings. On **love**, see notes at 6:27. (VII, VIII)

[36] Matthew 5:48 has "be perfect" for **be merciful**. Luke states even more basically what the previous verse has said and what is the rationale for the entire paragraph. No man can fully exemplify God's mercy, but he lives under this ideal if he is in the kingdom.

The Sermon on the Plain: On Judging, 6:37-42 (Matt. 7:1-5; 15:14; 10:24f.)

[37] Matthew 7:1f. gives the statement regarding judging,

³⁸ give, and it will be given to you; good measure, pressed down, shaken together, running over, will be put into your lap. For the measure you give will be the measure you get back."

---

but the statement regarding condemning is unique to Luke. What constitutes judging, and from whom does the reciprocal judgment come? Regarding the first inquiry perhaps the meaning is to avoid judging motives, or to avoid censorious judgment (which is supported by **condemn** following), or to avoid acting as God in trying to pronounce a man's final standing before his Maker. Man is not good enough or wise enough to **judge**. Yet, the New Testament does allow admonition, as well as the statement of facts, even requiring them upon occasion (Acts 13:44ff.; Rom. 1:32; 1 Cor. 5:11ff.). The control is the motive of love, as indicated in the preceding part of Jesus' speech. If judgment is inevitable, it should be done with a redemptive motive (cf. Rom. 2:1; 14:4; James 4:10f.; 5:9).

Those who would **judge** the judger could include other people, who repay in kind the lovelessness shown them; or eventually, God himself.

Jesus, of course, was not forbidding the administration of justice in the courts (cf. Rom. 13:1-7). In the immediate context he might have referred to the "religious" people of the day who were uncharitable to the sinners (see 5:29-32; 7:39).

Receiving God's forgiveness is dependent upon a forgiving spirit toward others (see notes at 4:39) though, of course, men can never grant forgiveness perfectly as God can. Further, other men will be more prone to **forgive** one who has exhibited forgiveness to them (cf. Matt. 6:14; 18:32f.). (II, VIII)

[38] Love is to be without **measure**. The figure is probably taken from the measuring of grain. The **lap** was formed by a loose garment overhanging a girdle, which was often used as a pocket (see Ruth 3:15). Men will generally treat

LUKE 6:38-41 — *Blind Leaders*

³⁹ He also told them a parable: "Can a blind man lead a blind man? Will they not both fall into a pit? ⁴⁰ A disciple is not above his teacher, but everyone when he is fully taught will be like his teacher. ⁴¹ Why do you see the speck that is in your brother's eye, but do not notice the log that is in your own eye?

---

another as they are treated. Even more, God will give without **measure** if one loves others without **measure**. And God has a larger **measure** than man! The effect of Christian love in a person's life is in proportion to his practice of it. It is a striking figure of how men of the kingdom are to spend themselves for others. Yet, Jesus' disciples do not **give**, or forgive just for what they hope to receive in return, for this would defeat the entire ethic of the Lord. (VIII)

[39] Both unwalled open wells and unfenced quarries were numerous in Palestine. The literal meaning of Jesus' words is clear. The application is a bit more difficult. In Matthew 15:14 it referred to the Pharisees. Here it might mean that one could not teach others if unwilling to learn from Jesus. To learn and do his teachings would keep one from being a blind leader, taking people to their destruction. A true disciple and leader must first reform his own life. Jesus paints a humorous picture of an untaught person or hypocrite trying to lead others.

[40] This proverbial saying means the same as the other aphorisms in the context: Do not exalt yourself! Disciples can get no nearer truth than the teacher brings them, so they should recognize their true position as learners.

[41] Matthew's parallel in 7:1-5 is in the context of not judging. Here the subjects of the preceding verses (judging and responsibilities of learners) are tied together. The **speck** could refer to anything small and dry, as chips, twigs, or bits of wood. **Notice** indicates prolonged attention or observation. **The log** was a bearing, or main beam, which received the other beams in a roof or floor.

Jesus' Humor   LUKE 6:42-45

⁴² Or how can you say to your brother, 'Brother, let me take out the speck that is in your eye,' when you yourself do not see the log that is in your own eye? You hypocrite, first take the log out of your own eye, and then you will see clearly to take out the speck that is in your brother's eye.

⁴³ "For no good tree bears bad fruit, nor again does a bad tree bear good fruit; ⁴⁴for each tree is known by its own fruit. For figs are not gathered from thorns, nor are grapes picked from a bramble bush. ⁴⁵ The good man out of the good treasure of his heart produces good, and the evil man out of his evil treasure produces evil; for out of the abundance of the heart his mouth speaks.

---

[42] Jesus, in this imagery, which was also used by the rabbis, again shows his sense of humor. One can hardly imagine even having a beam in one's eye, much less being so oblivious to it that one would notice another man's **speck**. Further, it is ridiculous to see such a person getting close enough to the other to practice removal of a **speck**. The bizarre nature of Jesus' picture would force thought and reflection, which was what he intended. Jesus is saying that one who would not practice self-investigation and correction before becoming a teacher would be a blind guide. One cannot assess the lives of others until assessing one's own.

The Sermon on the Plain: A Test of Goodness, 6:43-46 (Matt. 7:16-21; 12:33-35)

[43, 44] These verses further amplify the general idea of verses 39f. **Bad fruit** translates a Greek word indicating something rotten, putrid, and worthless. A life cannot effectively be on the outside what it is not on the inside. Jesus desires internal devotion and external practice, not just the latter divorced from the former.

[45] Jesus now passes to the basic principle that informs a person's life. A man's badness or goodness comes from his **heart**. This verse applies the illustration of the preceding

LUKE 6:45 — 7:2 — *Doers of the Word*

⁴⁶"Why do you call me 'Lord, Lord' and not do what I tell you? ⁴⁷Every one who comes to me and hears my words and does them, I will show you what he is like: ⁴⁸he is like a man building a house, who dug deep, and laid the foundation upon rock; and when a flood arose, the stream broke against that house, and could not shake it, because it had been well built.ʷ ⁴⁹But he who hears and does not do them is like a man who built a house on the ground without a foundation; against which the stream broke, and immediately it fell, and the ruin of that house was great."

¹After he had ended all his sayings in the hearing of the people he entered Capernaum.

ʷ Other ancient authorities read *founded upon the rock*

---

and also forms a link to the next section, which is a saying of direct application to Jesus' hearers.

[46] This verse ties together the entire section from 39-46, especially catching up the idea of verses 42 and 45 regarding the theme of "being" versus "pretending" or "saying" (cf. Matt. 21:28-32; James 1:22-25). Normally acknowledgment of lordship implies obedience, but there may have been followers who enjoyed the miracles and the teaching but had not yet become serious enough to render full discipleship. (VI)

The Sermon on the Plain: Hearers and Doers of the Word, 6:47-49 (Matt. 7:24-27)

[47-49] The picture is of a flash **flood** of a river. The key word is **foundation**. The crises of life will show the real nature of one's discipleship. Only hearing Jesus' teachings would not sustain one, but being the kind of person he depicted would. **The ruin** would be **great**, because it symbolized **the ruin** of a person. (VI)

The Centurion's Slave, 7:1-10 (Matt. 8:5-13; cf. also John 4:46-53)

[1, 2] Luke's account lays greater stress on the character

A Centurion
LUKE 7:2-7

²Now a centurion had a slave who was dear[x] to him, who was sick and at the point of death. ³When he heard of Jesus, he sent to him elders of the Jews, asking him to come and heal his slave. ⁴And when they came to Jesus, they besought him earnestly, saying, "He is worthy to have you do this for him, ⁵for he loves our nation, and he built us our synagogue." ⁶And Jesus went with them. When he was not far from the house, the centurion sent friends to him, saying to him, "Lord, do not trouble yourself, for I am not worthy to have you come under my roof; ⁷therefore I did not presume to come to you. But say the word, and let my servant be healed.

[x] Or *valuable*

---

of the soldier than Matthew does. The story shows how a Gentile could share in the blessings of the Lord. A **centurion** commanded approximately one hundred soldiers (either Romans or native troops). Such men are often mentioned kindly in the New Testament (cf. Luke 23:47; Acts 10:1; 27:43). Here his compassion for his slave was to his credit. This man probably accepted the principles and teachings of Judaism, though he had not become a full convert (note vs. 5).

[3] Verses 3-5 are unique to Luke. Matthew says the centurion himself came to **Jesus**, whereas in Luke he never sees the Lord. Perhaps Luke gives the more specific account, while Matthew simply generalizes. **Elders** were community leaders, and the centurion may have thought they would have more influence with Jesus. It is a tribute to the soldier that they were willing to go, especially when there was often hostility between the Jews and Romans (in particular Roman soldiers).

[4, 5] Again the details enhance the centurion's character. The elders may have thought Jesus shared the common Jewish prejudices regarding Romans, so they appealed to him earnestly. The soldier had probably subsidized the building of the **synagogue**. On love see notes at 6:27. (VI)

[6, 7] Perhaps **the centurion** did not come personally

LUKE 7:7-12 — Great Faith

⁸"For I am a man set under authority, with soldiers under me: and I say to one, 'Go,' and he goes; and to another, 'Come,' and he comes; and to my slave, 'Do this,' and he does it." ⁹When Jesus heard this, he marveled at him, and turned and said to the multitude that followed him, "I tell you, not even in Israel have I found such faith." ¹⁰And when those who had been sent returned to the house, they found the slave well.

¹¹Soon afterward[y] he went to a city called Nain, and his disciples and a great crowd went with him. ¹²As he drew near to the gate of the city, behold, a man who had died

---
[y] Other ancient authorities read *Next day*

---

because of his respect for the Jewish reluctance to associate with Gentiles and enter their houses (see Acts 11:3 and cf. Acts 16:15). The man was possessed of remarkable humility with his faith (contrast his **not worthy** with the Jews calling him "worthy" in vs. 4).

[8] He believed that the power of Jesus could transcend spatial and temporal barriers (see 4:6). A healing in such case would be remarkably impressive, and no possible accusation of trickery could be made. It took great faith to believe that Jesus could control illness as easily as the centurion could control his minions. He said, in effect, "I command **my slave**, but you command his illness." (VI)

[9, 10] The first incident after Jesus gives the kingdom teachings (6:20-49) shows a Gentile exhibiting the sort of **faith** that would make one a member of it. (VIII) Only twice did Jesus commend a remarkable faith and both instances were Gentiles (here and in Matt. 15:21-28; Mark 7:24-30; but cf. Luke 8:42-48). The centurion's **faith** is emphasized even more by Luke's reference to Jesus' marveling.

The Widow's Son at Nain, 7:11-17

[11, 12] Here Jesus is shown as the one who can overcome death, and the story thus stands as prelude to his

Raising the Widow's Son   LUKE 7:12-16

was being carried out, the only son of his mother, and she was a widow; and a large crowd from the city was with her. ¹³ And when the Lord saw her, he had compassion on her and said to her, "Do not weep." ¹⁴ And he came and touched the bier, and the bearers stood still. And he said, "Young man, I say to you, arise." ¹⁵ And the dead man sat up, and began to speak. And he gave him to his mother. ¹⁶ Fear seized them all; and they glorified God, saying, "A great prophet has arisen among us!" and "God has visited his people!"

---

resurrection (see also Mark 5:21-24, 35-43; John 11:1-44; 1 Kings 17:17-24; 2 Kings 4:32-37). This story is unique to Luke. **Nain**, mentioned only here in the Bible, was five miles southeast of Nazareth and overlooked the valley of Jezreel. The **mother** would have walked in front of the bier (a long wicker basket), so the Lord naturally addressed her first. **A widow** could be placed in dire straits, and if this woman were left without other relatives no one would be legally bound to support her. Also, the cutting off of the family line, if such were the case, would make this an unusually sad funeral (cf. 9:38f.). (VI)

[13, 14] This is one of the few places where **compassion** is noted as the specific motivation for a miracle (cf. 10:33). Because he was absolutely sure of what he could do, Jesus could say, **do not weep** (see Rev. 5:5; cf. Luke 23:28). **He touched the bier**: a custom which seems to have originated in the Elijah-Elisha healings (1 Kings 17:21; 2 Kings 4:34; 13:21; cf. also Luke 8:46). In the address to the **man**, the **you** was emphatic.

[15, 16] **The man** was given **to his mother**, reminiscent of 1 Kings 17:24. In this case, Jesus did not ask **the man** to follow him, perhaps due to the mother's need for her son's sustenance. Here was the first popular recognition of Jesus as **a prophet**, perhaps because of the Elijianic association of the miracle. Also, this was one of the messianic signs (7:22; see notes at 1:70; also Matt. 16:14; 21:46; Mark 6:15; Luke 7:39; 24:19; John 7:52). (IV)

LUKE 7:17-22 — *John's Question*

¹⁷ And this report concerning him spread through the whole of Judea and all the surrounding country.

¹⁸ The disciples of John told him of all these things. ¹⁹ And John, calling to him two of his disciples, sent them to the Lord, saying, "Are you he who is to come, or shall we look for another?" ²⁰ And when the men had come to him, they said, "John the Baptist has sent us to you, saying, 'Are you he who is to come, or shall we look for another?'" ²¹ In that hour he cured many of diseases and plagues and evil spirits and on many that were blind he bestowed sight. ²² And he answered them, "Go and tell John what you have seen and heard: the blind receive their sight, the lame walk, lepers are cleansed, and the deaf hear, the dead are raised up, the poor have good news preached to them.

---

[17] On the **spread** of Jesus' fame see 4:14, 37; 5:17. This notoriety would explain one reason John's disciples would have heard of his works. (VI)

John's Question to Jesus, 7:18-35 (Matt. 11:1-19).

This episode has three parts: verses 18-23 are the Baptist's question and its answer, 24-28 describe his role in redemptive history, and 29-35 give the meaning of his rejection by the nation.

[18, 19] **He who is to come** was based on Malachi 3:1 (see Luke 7:27). Was Jesus, the Elijianic healer, the Elijah foretold by Malachi, who would **come** with judgment (Mal. 3:2-4; 4:5f.)? In response to this implied meaning of John's question, Jesus interpreted his mission in terms, not of Malachi, but of the servant of the Lord concept of Isaiah (42:6f.; and cf. 29:18f.; 35:5f.; 61:1) and hoped John would not take offense (vs. 23).

[20-22] Jesus answered by deeds rather than words. Compare the similarities with Luke 4:18f., as well as the Isaiah passages listed there. Jesus gave no signs of a physical

John's Importance   LUKE 7:22-27

²³ And blessed is he who takes no offense at me."

²⁴ When the messengers of John had gone, he began to speak to the crowds concerning John: "What did you go out into the wilderness to behold? A reed shaken by the wind? ²⁵ What then did you go out to see? A man clothed in soft raiment? Behold, those who are gorgeously appareled and live in luxury are in king's courts. ²⁶ What then did you go out to see? A prophet? Yes, I tell you, and more than a prophet. ²⁷ This is he of whom it is written,

'Behold, I send my messenger before thy face,
who shall prepare thy way before thee.'

---

kingdom but did appeal to John and his disciples to believe because the purposes of God were being realized. Luke has previously referred to cures of **the blind** (vs. 21) and **lepers** (5:12-16); **the dead raised** (7:11-17); and perhaps to **the lame** walking (5:17-26, though the primary disease was paralysis). In the Old Testament passages leprosy and resurrection were not mentioned as signs to be done. It is interesting that the preaching to **the poor** was as much a messianic sign as the others (on preaching **good news**, see notes at 1:19). (VI, VIII)

[23] The **offense** implied the idea of being tripped up, or trapped. It probably indicates that John's concept of Messiah was different from Jesus' presentation, and John should not be offended at this correction. (IV, VI, VII)

[24, 25] These are Jesus' first words about **John** in Luke (but cf. 1:17), and he is more complimentary than one might have supposed from his previous remarks. His words indicate they went **out to** find something that was not to be found elsewhere and which was definitely worth finding.

[26] Jesus progressed in his description from reed, to man, to **prophet**, to **more than a prophet**. He endorsed John's task and now shows its further implications.

[27] Here Jesus explains how John was more (vs. 26). He would **prepare** the way for the Lord in a way no prophet

LUKE 7:27-30 *John's Importance*

²⁸ I tell you, among those born of women none is greater than John; yet he who is least in the kingdom of God is greater than he." ²⁹ (When they heard this all the people and the tax collectors justified God, having been baptized with the baptism of John; ³⁰ but the Pharisees and the lawyers rejected the purpose of God for themselves, not having been baptized by him.)

---

had done. John was the Elijianic figure, according to this citation from Malachi 3:1 (see Mal. 4:5f.). So John, in a sense, fulfilled the passage he expected Jesus to fulfill (see discussion vs. 19). The Malachi citation as given here is in a form different from either the Hebrew or Septuagint text. This form may have been one that had become stereotyped before the evangelists used it, since they all agree in the differences (Matt. 11:10; Mark 1:2). Perhaps, on the basis of similarity with Exodus 23:20, Jesus was linking the exodus and prophetic salvation themes. This is the second time in Luke that Jesus has given an interpretation of scripture (see 4:18; also 24:27, 45). (VII)

[28] Though in some sense the prophets were **in the kingdom** (13:28), yet **John** was not during his lifetime, since **the kingdom** had not yet fully arrived. Thus Jesus stressed the greatness of **the kingdom** (see notes at 1:33).

[29, 30] This saying is likely from Luke, inserted here to explicate the context. It gives insight into the way he saw the ministry of **John**. The contrast is between those justifying **God** in verse 29 and those rejecting his **purpose** in verse 30 (cf. a similar polarity regarding Jesus in verses 36-50). To justify **God** meant they accepted what **God** did through **John**, with his preaching of judgment and repentance as indications of the imminent kingdom (see the idea of justifying **God** as holding him to be right, *Psalms of Solomon* 2:15; 3:3, 5; 4:8). According to one translation, they "acknowledged God's plan." The verb for **rejected** is a strong one. Their refusal of **baptism** not only implied unwillingness to repent but also constituted a rejection of God's actions in bringing the kingdom.

Human Inconsistency   **LUKE 7:31-35**

³¹ "To what then shall I compare the men of this generation, and what are they like? ³² They are like children sitting in the market place and calling to one another,
'We piped to you, and you did not dance;
we wailed, and you did not weep.'
³³ For John the Baptist has come eating no bread and drinking no wine; and you say, 'He has a demon.' ³⁴ The Son of man has come eating and drinking; and you say, 'Behold, a glutton and a drunkard, a friend of tax collectors and sinners!' ³⁵ Yet wisdom is justified by all her children."

[31, 32] The idea here is of people who will not be satisfied regardless of how they are approached. Previous criticisms by Jesus of the religious insensitivity of the people are found in 4:23ff.; 5:23f., 31f.; 6:3-5, 7.

[33] John's habits and these reactions to him are not revealed elsewhere. Refusal of **wine** (see 1:15) may suggest a Nazirite vow. John's abstinence was attributed to **demon** possession. In addition to unconventional behavior (cf. Matt. 11:18; Mark 3:22; Luke 8:27), **demon** possession was appealed to also to explain attitudes considered basically false (John 7:20; 10:20). This accusation was a way in which those who could not bear the truth of his message could outwardly evade responsibility.

[34] These charges against Jesus were not true, though related to actual facts. Jesus did drink wine and did eat with **tax collectors and sinners** (cf. 5:29-32), but he was no **glutton** and **drunkard**. These comparisons may imply some significant difference between the missions of Jesus and John. On **Son of man**, see notes at 5:24. (IV)

[35] **Children** of wisdom (cf. Prov. 1:20; 8:22), or of the all-wise God, appreciate and welcome God's words. They see what things are really important (as verses 36-50 will show). They are those who justify God (vs. 29), in contrast to those who reject him (vs. 30), or refuse to be pleased by anything (vss. 32-34). (VI)

LUKE 7:36-38 — *A Pharisee's Dinner*

³⁶ One of the Pharisees asked him to eat with him, and he went into the Pharisee's house, and sat at a table. ³⁷ And behold, a woman of the city, who was a sinner, when she learned that he was sitting at table in the Pharisee's house, brought an alabaster flask of ointment, ³⁸ and standing behind him at his feet, weeping, she began to wet his feet with her tears, and wiped them with the hair of her head, and kissed his feet, and anointed them with the ointment.

The Woman with the Ointment, 7:36-50

[36] Some have identified this story with Matthew 26:6-13; Mark 14:3-9; and John 12:3-8, but there are too many differences for such an identification to be made. Not least among them is the contrast between the character of the woman here and Mary in the other story. Similarities may be due to the two stories interacting on each other in the telling. The present story is powerfully descriptive, elaborating by a concrete case the principles expressed by Jesus in verses 29-35. The motives for the **Pharisee's** invitation might possibly have been curiosity, because he conceded that Jesus might be a prophet. From the lack of hospitality shown Jesus, it is doubtful the meal was intended to pay great honor to him. Guests at the meal reclined on low couches, leaning on the left arm and keeping the right free. On meals, see notes at 5:29.

[37, 38] This **woman** was probably a harlot, though she could have been the wife of an irreligious person. She had probably had previous contact with Jesus, and the experience had led her to profound repentance. In the East, houses seemed somewhat open to intrusion of this sort (see Matt. 9:10; Luke 5:29f. and discussion there). But of all the places such **a woman** might go, a **Pharisee's house** would seem the most unlikely. Her appearance occasioned some surprise (note **behold**). Common opinions of her could not be high. The experience may have been even more embarrassing if Jesus were in a prominent place at the meal. Perhaps

The Sinful Woman LUKE 7:38-40

³⁹ Now when the Pharisee who had invited him saw it, he said to himself, "If this man were a prophet, he would have known who and what sort of woman this is who is touching him, for she is a sinner." ⁴⁰ And Jesus answering said to him, "Simon, I have something to say to you." And he answered, "What is it, Teacher?"

---

the **woman** only intended to anoint his **feet**, but out of gratitude she was overcome by her emotions and extended her ministrations (cf. 5:32). At meals the sandals were removed, and in her trauma she wept upon **his feet** and laved them in **her tears**, in addition to anointing them **with the ointment** from the **alabaster flask** (the term was used of boxes and phials even when they were not actually **alabaster**). To the Jews it was shameful for **a woman to** let down her **hair** in public. A Jewish girl would bind it up on her wedding day and never appear with it unbound. But this **woman** broke the custom, in what was perhaps a spontaneous action. Further devotion was shown in the kissing of the **feet**. The verb indicates a continual and affectionate kissing. It is the same used to describe the kiss of Judas Iscariot (22:47 — an ironic twist), that of the prodigal's father (15:20), and that of the Ephesian elders (Acts 20:37). (VI)

[39] **The Pharisee** had the conception that no religious person would allow such contact from **a sinner**. It would be a prophet's business to know whom the sinners were so they could be avoided (see 7:16). Obviously, then, Jesus could not be **a prophet**. Ironically, Jesus passes the Pharisee's test, for he did know who she was. But he denied the Pharisee's premise about the untouchability of such people. To further the irony, **the Pharisee** would discover Jesus knew what kind of man he was. He completely missed the real human drama that was taking place and the reason for the woman's emotion. (VI)

[40] Jesus read his mind (III), as he addressed **Simon**.

LUKE 7:40-46 *Forgiveness*

[41] "A certain creditor had two debtors; one owed five hundred denarii, and the other fifty. [42] When they could not pay, he forgave them both. Now which of them will love him more?" [43] Simon answered, "The one, I suppose, to whom he forgave more." And he said to him, "You have judged rightly." [44] Then turning toward the woman he said to Simon, "Do you see this woman? I entered your house, you gave me no water for my feet, but she has wet my feet with her tears and wiped them with her hair. [45] You gave me no kiss, but from the time I came in she has not ceased to kiss my feet. [46] You did not anoint my head with oil, but she has anointed my feet with ointment.

His request to speak would attract greater attention to what he was to say.

[41, 42] The silver denarius was a basic unit of Roman coinage. In some cases it was a day's wage (Matt. 20:2), so that the contrast would be **fifty** days' salary versus that for about a year and a third. The creditor's forgiveness was a demonstration of genuine grace (cf. Matt. 18:27). In both cases it was total, but the response varied with the amount forgiven. Gratitude was probably in proportion to the debtor's estimate of the amount and the difficulty of payment, rather than the actual sum. Both knew they were insolvent, but they could have felt it with varying degrees of keenness. On **love,** see notes at 6:27.

[43] Simon had fallen into Jesus' trap and admitted the validity of the point before Jesus had made the application (cf. 10:28). The implication of the story was that forgiveness preceded gratitude.

[44-46] The comparative behavior of **the woman** and the host offers an impressive contrast between true devotion and a certain rudeness. Perhaps **the woman** had sought for the chance to show her gratitude to the Lord, and Simon's lack of hospitality provided her opportunity to act. Such amenities as those indicated by Jesus were necessary because of the effect of wind and sun on the skin, as well

Love   LUKE 7:46-50

⁴⁷ Therefore I tell you, her sins, which are many, are forgiven, for she loved much; but he who is forgiven little, loves little." ⁴⁸ And he said to her, "Your sins are forgiven." ⁴⁹ Then those who were at table with him began to say among themselves, "Who is this, who even forgives sins?" ⁵⁰ And he said to the woman, "Your faith has saved you; go in peace."

---

as because traveling shod only in sandals would demand footwashing (on footwashing, cf. Gen. 18:4; John 13:5ff.; 1 Tim. 5:10). The **kiss** would be a courteous form of greeting. Luke does not say why **Simon** had ignored such hospitality. Perhaps he did favors only for those he felt could render him some service in return. But he would be expected to extend hospitality while no such social obligation lay on **the woman.**

Anointing was sometimes done with olive **oil,** but here it was the more expensive **ointment. The woman,** concerned with more than customary courtesies, was expressing true love. And it was no perfunctory act but a continuing devotion. **Simon** didn't even go through the ritual of unloving formalities. And later, he seemed to have felt no shame for his neglect. (VI)

[47, 48] Jesus certainly was not saying that her love earned her forgiveness, for that would contradict the whole point of his story. Faith saved her (vs. 50); the greatness of her love was proof of the greatness of her forgiveness. The reference to her **many sins** may be a reflection of Simon's opinion of her (on sins, see notes 1:77; 3:3). She knew the meaning of forgiveness, whereas the host did not. Simon certainly needed it but was insensitive to his need.

[49] Here is the second time in Luke Jesus is criticized for forgiving **sins** (see 5:20ff). Jesus' critics were not courageous enough to express their criticism openly. Perhaps they were rationalizing their failure to accept Jesus' point. (VI)

[50] Here again Jesus responded to what people were thinking, or at least what they were not openly expressing to him (III). **The woman** believed in what Jesus could do,

LUKE 7:50 — 8:2   *Mary Magdalene*

¹Soon afterward he went on through cities and villages, preaching and bringing the good news of the kingdom of God. And the twelve were with him, ²and also some women who had been healed of evil spirits and infirmities: Mary, called Magdalene, from whom seven demons had gone out,

---

in sharp contrast to those in verse 49 who did not. In commending **the woman**, he was probably implying they lacked what she had, i.e., **faith** (see notes at 5:20; and cf. Matt. 9:22; Mark 10:52; Luke 17:19; 18:42; Rom. 10:9). On **peace**, see notes at 1:79. (II)

The Ministering Women, 8:1-3, (Matt. 4:23; 9:35)

[1] The present section (especially 8:4-21), along with 6:20-49, is one of the collections of teachings prior to the main body of teaching material in the book (9:51—18:14). These three verses prepare the reader for the parable of the sower, to follow. On **preaching**, see notes at 1:19; on **kingdom**, see notes at 1:33.

[2] This section indicates the importance of **women** in Luke's presentation of the gospel (see notes at 1:5; and cf. Acts 1:14, 21f.). It is possible that the **women** specifically named may have been known by Luke's readers. It seems unusual that they would travel with this group. They did provide finances (also unusual), but their other reasons are not given. Perhaps it was their devotion to Jesus, in some cases intensified by his healing of them. It is not necessary that all of these **women** were in the company all of the time.

Mary's **seven demons** may indicate her possession was of extraordinary malignity. Some would even see it as indicating a series of relapses. On Mary's devotion to Jesus see Mark 15:40f.; 16:1; Luke 23:55-24:11; John 19:25; 20:11-20. Magdala, a predominantly Gentile town, was at the south end of the plain of Gennesaret. There is no indication Jesus was ever there, though he was in the area (Matt. 14:34; Mark 6:53).

The Sower LUKE 8:3-6

³and Joanna, the wife of Chuza, Herod's steward, and Susanna, and many others, who provided for them ⸱ out of their means.
⁴And when a great crowd came together and people from town after town came to him, he said in a parable: ⁵"A sower went out to sow his seed; and as he sowed, some fell along the path, and was trodden under foot, and the birds of the air devoured it. ⁶And some fell on the rock; and as it grew up, it withered away, because it had no moisture.

⸱ Other ancient authorities read *him*

---

[3] Jesus was apparently willing to accept this help. Though he had the power, he did not work miracles to insure his physical support (but see the feedings of the five thousand and the four thousand). **Susanna** is not mentioned elsewhere in the New Testament, and **Joanna** only in 24:10. **Chuza**, Joanna's husband, was perhaps a domestic administrator. Herod was probably Antipas. The influence of Jesus had penetrated even the court of the ruler. (VI, VIII)

The Parable of the Sower, 8:4-8 (Matt. 13:1-9; Mark 4:1-9)

[4, 5] This parable, in comparing something commonly known with the not so well known, had the effect of sifting Jesus' followers to see which were genuine. The farmer, broadcasting **his seed**, was a common scene. **The path** would be packed and hard, not allowing the **seed** to germinate. There is a graphic change of prepositions in this parable, moving from **along the path**, to "on the rock," to "among thorns," to "into good soil."

[6] The reference is to a substratum of **rock** covered by a layer of soil which would allow growth but which would dry quickly in the sun. The plants, unable to penetrate **the rock** to find **moisture**, would wither. Yet from the surface, before the soil dried, these plants would look the same as others.

LUKE 8:7-11 *Purpose of Parables*

⁷And some fell among thorns; and the thorns grew with it and choked it. ⁸And some fell into good soil and grew, and yielded a hundredfold." As he said this, he called out, "He who has ears to hear, let him hear."

⁹And when his disciples asked him what this parable meant, ¹⁰he said, "To you it has been given to know the secrets of the kingdom of God; but for others they are in parables, so that seeing they may not see, and hearing they may not understand. ¹¹Now the parable is this: The seed is the word of God.

[7, 8] He who has ears to hear may mean, "Listen, this is important!" Or, more probably, it was a call for right understanding of the deeper meaning of the parable and, consequently, of Jesus' teachings (see 8:18).

The Reason for Speaking in Parables, 8:9, 10 (Matt. 13:10-15; Mark 4:10-12)

[9, 10] This question came, according to Mark, when Jesus was alone. His answer divides the **disciples** from those who are "outside" (Mark), yet both groups require further understanding (see Isa. 6:9f.; Jer. 5:21; Ezek. 12:2). The **parable** form kept some people from **seeing**, because they did not want to. For those that did want to know, the lesson was made even clearer. In either case the willingness or unwillingness to think would divide true followers from others. Further, what the unsympathetic would hear without understanding they would remember because of its form, and it might be that later they would come to grasp the meaning. The **parable**, concealing and revealing, becomes a sign of judgment—against unbelief. **(V)** On **kingdom**, see notes at 1:33.

The Interpretation of the Parable of the Sower, 8:11-15 (Matt. 13:18-23; Mark 4:13-20)

[11-15] Luke, apparently interested in the fact of

Interpretation LUKE 8:11-17

¹²The ones along the path are those who have heard; then the devil comes and takes away the word from their hearts, that they may not believe and be saved. ¹³And the ones on the rock are those who, when they hear the word, receive it with joy; but these have no root, they believe for a while and in time of temptation fall away. ¹⁴And as for what fell among the thorns, they are those who hear, but as they go on their way they are choked by the cares and riches and pleasures of life, and their fruit does not mature. ¹⁵And as for that in the good soil, they are those who, hearing the word, hold it fast in an honest and good heart, and bring forth fruit with patience.

¹⁶No one after lighting a lamp covers it with a vessel, or puts it under a bed, but puts it on a stand, that those who enter may see the light. ¹⁷For nothing is hid that shall not be made manifest, nor anything secret that shall not be known and come to light.

---

productivity, not degrees of it, omits the one hundred, sixty, and thirty-fold of Matthew and Mark. Those who accept and enter the kingdom will find the procedure fruitful. **Honest and good** (cf. Matt. 7:21-23) repeats the Greek description of a true gentleman. It may be that Luke was especially concerned to encourage his own audience to help them deal with setbacks in their faith. (II, V, VI, VIII)

The Purpose of Parables, 8:16-18 (Mark 4:21-25; cf. also Matt. 5:15; 13:12)

[16] What is meant to illumine must not be hidden, as Jesus humorously points out. **The light** Jesus kindled within the disciples must not be hid, either by failure in conduct or, especially, in proclamation.

[17] Compare a similar saying in Matthew 10:26 and Luke 12:2. The **secret** probably ties to the "secrets" of verse 10. Parables may seem obscure, but the truth they

LUKE 8:17-21   *Hear and Do*

[18] Take heed then how you hear; for to him who has will more be given, and from him who has not, even what he thinks that he has will be taken away."

[19] Then his mother and his brothers came to him, but they could not reach him for the crowd. [20] And he was told, "Your mother and your brothers are standing outside, desiring to see you." [21] But he said to them, "My mother and my brothers are those who hear the word of God and do it."

---

teach will become **known** in time. As a light must be in the open to do its work, so the gospel must **be known**, and then will do what it is intended to do. (V)

[18] There are similar expressions in Matthew 25:29; Luke 19:26, and the parallels listed. The man **who has not** is also the man who does not want. Spiritual pursuits would multiply blessings, whereas benefits selfishly acquired would eventually be lost. (VI)

Jesus' True Relatives, 8:19-21 (Matt. 12:46-50; Mark 3:31-35)

[19-21] For a similar saying see Luke 11:27f. Luke locates the saying here in order to fortify the point about the proper sort of hearing and response to God.

This is Luke's initial introduction to Jesus' **brothers** (see Mark 6:3) and the first mention of **his mother** since chapter two. Some think that Joseph died early in Jesus' life and that Jesus had to support the family, but Luke 4:22 may argue against this. According to John 7:5 (cf. Mark 3:21) Jesus' **brothers** were skeptical and did not believe in him during his life (but see Acts 1:14). This being the case, perhaps they **came** sign seeking, and Jesus' answer about the necessity of obedience was an admonition to all who might have come for the same motives. The point is that spiritual kinship is more important than physical relations (cf. Luke 14:25ff.). Also, physical kinship alone would not guarantee entrance into the kingdom of God (cf. Rom. 8:29; Heb. 2:11). (VI)

Calming The Storm   LUKE 8:21-25

> [22] One day he got into a boat with his disciples, and he said to them, "Let us go across to the other side of the lake." So they set out, [23] and as they sailed he fell asleep. And a storm of wind came down on the lake, and they were filling with water, and were in danger. [24] And they went and woke him, saying, "Master, Master, we are perishing!" And he awoke and rebuked the wind and the raging waves; and they ceased, and there was a calm. [25] He said to them, "Where is your faith?" And they were afraid, and they marveled, saying one to another, "Who then is this, that he commands even wind and water, and they obey him?"

The Stilling of the Storm, 8:22-25 (Matt. 8:18; Mark 4:35-41)

[22-24] With this story (and through 9:17) Luke returns to an outline of events identical to Mark. It is quite understandable that Jesus would be exhausted, so he slept, trusting the boatsmen and the care of God. The Sea of Galilee was subject to sudden and violent storms, which would sweep down through the ravines bordering the water. Such a squall hit so intensely that the boat was swamping. Jesus, exhausted, still slept, till he was awakened. Each of the gospels, in reporting the words of the disciples, uses a different word of address. In Mark it is teacher (*didaskale*); in Matthew lord (*kurie*); and in Luke **master** (*epistata*).

The word for **calm,** though common elsewhere, is used only here in the New Testament and makes the wonder more impressive, since normally the sea would continue to churn after a storm. Fishermen would especially notice this. Jesus, then, spoke to nature as to a rebellious child, and it obeyed him.

[25] In all Jesus exhibited a transcendent calm. The reason he rebuked their lack of **faith** (note 5:20) is not completely clear. Perhaps it was for not trusting that he could provide for them, as 5:10 indicated he could; or perhaps because they had inadequate **faith** in what he could do even

LUKE 8:25-28 — *Gerasene Demoniac*

²⁶ Then they arrived at the country of the Gerasenes,ᵃ which is opposite Galilee. ²⁷ And as he stepped out on land, there met him a man from the city who had demons; for a long time he had worn no clothes, and he lived not in a house but among the tombs. ²⁸ When he saw Jesus, he cried out and fell down before him, and said with a loud voice, "What have you to do with me, Jesus, Son of the Most High God? I beseech you, do not torment me."

ᵃ Other ancient authorities read *Gadarenes*, others *Gergesenes*

---

after they woke him. In either case, Jesus was helping them to develop the sort of trust they would sorely need in the future. This miracle impressed the disciples even more deeply than before. Here was something that could not be duplicated by wandering healers and exorcists, who might seem to have healed as Jesus had. Their reaction shows how the disciples were still formulating their opinion of Jesus. (IV, VI)

The Gerasene Demoniac, 8:26-39 (Matt. 8:28-34; Mark 5:1-20)

[26] This is the first trans-Galilean incident recorded by Luke. A glance at the variants in the footnote indicates the difficulty in locating this place. There is really no certainty as to the locale. It would, obviously, be somewhere along the seashore.

[27] Matthew indicates two demoniacs, while Mark and Luke speak of one, perhaps the more prominent of the two. The **demons** seem to have produced insanity, with its several symptoms. It was not unusual in Jewish and Greek literature to find evil spirits showing a predilection for such places as this man frequented.

[28] Mark says the man **saw Jesus** from afar and ran and worshiped him. Luke's readers knew mental disorders could have psychological and organic causes, so he makes it clear here that there was yet another cause. The demons, it would

Legion

29 For he had commanded the unclean spirit to come out of the man. (For many a time it had seized him; he was kept under guard, and bound with chains and fetters, but he broke the bonds and was driven by the demon into the desert.) 30 Jesus then asked him, "What is your name?" And he said, "Legion"; for many demons had entered him. 31 And they begged him not to command them to depart into the abyss.

---

seem, addressed **Jesus** through their host, recognizing him and also knowing he had power to **torment** them (see 4:34, 41). (IV, VI)

[29] Apparently Jesus had already spoken the word of exorcism, so the demons begged for leniency. Luke then reviews the man's state under this baleful influence. The seizures were frequent. The word for **seized** is only in Luke. **Many a time** may indicate, though the possession could have been permanent, that there were spasmodic periods of greater affliction. One manifestation was abnormal strength, so that the man would break the **chains** by which he would be held.

[30] Jesus' question may have been to recall the man to a sense of his personal identity, so he would know he and the evil powers within him were not the same. He may also, by establishing the severity of the possession, have hoped to build the faith of his disciples as they had witnessed the exorcism. The man's answer may indicate that he was so tormented that he could only cry out in terms of his affliction; or it may mean that the **demons** controlled and answered, as the expression for "we are many" (Mark) may indicate. A **Legion** was an army unit containing four to six thousand soldiers. Instead of taking the term to refer to a specific number of **demons,** it may indicate the severity of the affliction (as if that many spirits possessed the man's body).

[31] The demons recognized that when Jesus commanded, they must obey, and that **the abyss** was the fate for which they were destined (cf. Rev. 9:1-11; 11:7; 17:8;

LUKE 8:31-35 *The Swine*

³² Now a large herd of swine was feeding there on the hillside; and they begged him to let them enter these. So he gave them leave. ³³ Then the demons came out of the man and entered the swine, and the herd rushed down the steep bank into the lake and were drowned.

³⁴ When the herdsmen saw what had happened, they fled, and told it in the city and in the country. ³⁵ Then people went out to see what had happened, and they came to Jesus, and found the man from whom the demons had gone, sitting at the feet of Jesus, clothed and in his right mind; and they were afraid.

20:1-3). **The abyss** symbolized the chaos in opposition to which the world was fashioned (Gen. 1:2) and by which it was ever threatened. Jesus brought deliverance from this threat by sending the demons back to their realm. (VI)

[32, 33] The herd numbered about two thousand (Mark). Their action would give decisive evidence of the exorcism. Not all **the swine** were necessarily affected. If some of them began their rush to the sea, **the entire herd** may have been stampeded to follow. (IV) How could Jesus sanction such destruction, when the livelihood of so many people would be threatened? There are several possible solutions: (1) The act involved the inexplicable mystery of evil in the world. (2) Since all things are ultimately God's, he was free to do as he wished. (3) The event was necessary to demonstrate the reality and completeness of the cure, and animals could be sacrificed for the sake of the salvation of a human. (4) The keepers were Jews, herding pigs in violation of the law. The second suggestion seems best, but it is really impossible to give full consideration to the ethical problem, not knowing the further consequences of this loss. This and the destruction of the fig tree (Matt. 21:18-22; Mark 11:12-14, 20-25) are the only two incidents in Jesus' ministry where property was destroyed. (VI)

[34, 35] Were **the herdsmen** more concerned with what

The Cured Man　　　　　　　　　　　　LUKE 8:35-39

³⁶And those who had seen it told them how he who had been possessed with demons was healed. ³⁷Then all the people of the surrounding country of the Gerasenes *ᵃ* asked him to depart from them; for they were seized with great fear; so he got into the boat and returned. ³⁸The man from whom the demons had gone begged that he might be with him; but he sent him away, saying, ³⁹"Return to your home, and declare how much God has done for you." And he went away, proclaiming throughout the whole city how much Jesus had done for him.

ᵃ Other ancient authorities read *Gadarenes*, others *Gergesenes*

---

happened to the man or to the pigs, as they spread the news? Here, also, **Jesus** drew crowds of **people.** They came before he entered any **city** or had done any preaching. They apparently recognized **the man.** His demeanor, portrayed so graphically by Luke, shows markedly the contrast between the demon's and the Lord's influence on him (freed; **sitting** rather than restless; no longer anti-social; **clothed; in his right mind**).

The fearful reaction of the **people** ties this story to the preceding (vs. 25). Did they fear Jesus' special power, or **the** healed **man,** or the possibility of further economic loss (vs. 37)? On fear, see notes at 1:12.

[36, 37] The evidence of the event was augmented by the evidence of the eyewitnesses (had Luke known some of them?). Nowhere else in his ministry did Jesus receive a request **to depart.**

[38, 39] If **the man** was afraid he would be re-entered by **the demons,** the words of **Jesus** reassured him. Though elsewhere **Jesus** was loath to reveal his identity to the public (4:35, 41; 5:14; but cf. 7:22), he may have commanded **the man** to tell here because the declaration would not be of Jesus' identity but of his works. Or, Jesus' command may be explained by the possibility this was a heathen district; or the fact that **the man** would not be suited for work elsewhere; or the fact the miracle could not be used for

LUKE 8:38-43 — *Jairus*

⁴⁰Now when Jesus returned, the crowd welcomed him, for they were all waiting for him. ⁴¹And there came a man named Jairus, who was a ruler of the synagogue; and falling at Jesus' feet he besought him to come to his house, ⁴²for he had an only daughter, about twelve years of age, and she was dying.

As he went, the people pressed round him. ⁴³And a woman who had had a flow of blood for twelve years*ᵇ* and could not be healed by any one, ⁴⁴came up behind him, and touched the fringe of his garment; and immediately her flow of blood ceased.

ᵇ Other ancient authorities add *and had spent all her living upon physicians*

---

political purposes. Even though Jesus chose to leave without further activity in that area, much had been accomplished by the impact of the healing. The man who was made well would spread the word, and, in a sense, continue Jesus' ministry. (V, VI)

Jairus' Daughter and a Woman's Faith, 8:40-56 (Matt. 9:18-26; Mark 5:21-43)

[40-42] Here Luke gives the first of three stories involving the number **twelve** (through 9:6). Only Luke tells that **the crowd** was **waiting,** indicating they had fairly good knowledge of Jesus' movements. The people seemed to be wherever he went (see Mark 1:37). Many of them would ask for special attention. Perhaps this case is singled out because of its pathos. The **ruler** would probably be given more ready access to **Jesus** due to his position as the president of **the synagogue** who conducted service and selected participants. Apparently not all the religious leaders were hostile to **Jesus.** Only Luke notes the girl was Jairus' **only** child (see 7:12; 9:38). Matthew's account says the girl had died, whereas the present text says **she was dying.** Matthew may be telescoping events, since his account is briefer.

[43, 44] The hemorrhage may have been a continuous menstrual flow. Mark says she had suffered under many

A Woman Healed   LUKE 8:43-48

⁴⁵ And Jesus said, "Who was it that touched me?" When all denied it, Peter ᶜ said, "Master, the multitudes surround you and press upon you!" ⁴⁶ But Jesus said, "Some one touched me; for I perceive that power has gone forth from me." ⁴⁷ And when the woman saw that she was not hidden, she came trembling, and falling down before him declared in the presence of all the people why she had touched him, and how she had been immediately healed. ⁴⁸ And he said to her, "Daughter, your faith has made you well; go in peace."

<small>ᶜ Other ancient authorities add *and those who were with him*</small>

---

physicians (see footnote). Luke, perhaps because he was a doctor, has a different wording. The **flow of blood** would make the woman legally unclean (Lev. 15:19-30). Perhaps this is why she **came up behind** Jesus. Or she may have been embarrassed to declare publicly the nature of her illness. In Numbers 15:38-41 **the fringe** signified one's consecration to God. Perhaps that was the case with Jesus. (VI)

[45] **Jesus** stopped, since he knew that he could heal the daughter of Jairus at any time. He had doubtless willed the woman with the hemorrhage to be made well, but he wished her to avow her act, both so he could teach a lesson about faith and so the woman would be aware that she was no longer unclean. (III)

[46-48] Jesus' specific words (given only by Luke) indicate that he knew when he was healing the lady (unless one assumes that **power** went out involuntarily). **Jesus** distinguished this touch from others just because of what he had done with it. Luke gives a graphic picture of the woman's psychological response as she mustered her courage to declare herself. In the presence of Jesus' request and knowledge of the event, it would have been difficult to do otherwise. The implication is that **Jesus** knew of the woman's **faith** and so called her to give it public expression and teach a lesson (cf. 7:9; 8:25; 17:19; 18:42). On **peace,** see notes at 1:79; **faith,** see notes at 5:10. (VI)

LUKE 8:49-56 *Girl Raised*

⁴⁹ While he was still speaking, a man from the ruler's house came and said, "Your daughter is dead; do not trouble the Teacher any more." ⁵⁰ But Jesus on hearing this answered him, "Do not fear; only believe, and she shall be made well." ⁵¹ And when he came to the house, he permitted no one to enter with him, except Peter and John and James, and the father and mother of the child. ⁵² And all were weeping and bewailing her; but he said, "Do not weep; for she is not dead but sleeping." ⁵³ And they laughed at him, knowing that she was dead. ⁵⁴ But taking her by the hand he called, saying, "Child, arise." ⁵⁵ And her spirit returned, and she got up at once; and he directed that something should be given her to eat. ⁵⁶ And her parents were

---

[49, 50] All four miracle stories in this chapter of Luke note the idea of **fear**. The first, third, and fourth of them have the same indication of **fear** in Mark as well. The Greek places the word **dead** first to stress the point. **Jesus** could indeed heal, but the messenger would not imagine his raising the **dead**. Mark says **Jesus** ignored the messenger's words. One can imagine the chagrin of the anxious father as **Jesus** delayed while his **daughter** released her hold on life (cf. John 11:6). (VI)

[51, 52] Jesus' words to the grieving parents seemed so incongruous and presumptuous in their context that, had not **the child** been raised, they would have been most cruel (cf. notes 7:13). But from Jesus' perspective physical death was a no more serious barrier than waking someone from sleep. The event, a tremendous testimony to God's power, would have even larger significance when seen by the church in the light of Jesus' resurrection.

[53-56] The laughter of unbelief is opposed to the **do not weep** that called for faith. Mark says the people were put outside after their laughter. The Lord went in and touched her **hand**—even though contact with a corpse rendered one unclean (cf. the leper in 5:13). This in itself was mute

Climax of Ministry   LUKE 8:53-56

amazed; but he charged them to tell no one what had happened.

---

testimony to what he would do, since soon the regulation of the law would not apply. He spoke to the **child** as if gently waking her. He who casts out unclean spirits also brought back the child's spirit.

In their joy and amazement the parents had to be reminded to feed the **child**. Then, as before (see notes at 8:39), Jesus gave a prohibition regarding telling the news. Perhaps he desired that the details be kept secret, or, more likely, he wished as little publicity as possible, since he was already followed by such throngs. He was more concerned about learners and followers than simply sign seekers. (V, VI)

THE GALILEAN MINISTRY COMPLETED, 9:1-50

This section records the climax of Jesus' Galilean ministry. His ministry was extended through the twelve (1-6), and reactions to him reached a peak (7-9, 20), leading to Jesus' fuller revelation of himself (20-22, 28-36) and his passion sayings (22, 31, 44). The demands of discipleship become more stringent (23-27, 48) as the kingdom neared (27). Yet the disciples still did not understand (45).

There are a remarkable number of correspondences between this section and the passion narrative in 22:7-23:16. They are 9:1-6 with 22:35-38; 9:7-9 with 23:6-16; 9:10-17 with 22:7-19; 9:20 with 22:31-34; 9:23-27 with 22:28-30; 9:28-36 with 22:39-46; 9:37-43a with 22:47-53; 9:43b-45 with 22:21-23; and 9:46-48 with 22:24-27. It seems obvious Luke wishes the reader to associate these sections. Thus he is saying that the Jesus of the Galilean ministry (preaching and healing) is the same as the Jesus who died, arose, and ascended in Jerusalem. There is also a remarkable series of correspondences between Luke 9:1-50 and Acts 1, confirming the same point.

LUKE 9:1-3 — *Mission of the Twelve*

¹And he called the twelve together and gave them power and authority over all demons and to cure diseases, ²and he sent them out to preach the kingdom of God and to heal. ³And he said to them, "Take nothing for your journey, no staff, nor bag, nor bread, nor money; and do not have two tunics.

The Sending Out of the Twelve, 9:1-6 (Matt. 9:35; 10:1, 9-11, 14; Mark 6:6b-13)

[1, 2] The selection of **the twelve** was recorded in 6:12-16. The sending would prepare **them** for their post-ascension mission (see 5:10). They went **to preach the kingdom of God** (notes 1:33)—only to Israel, as Matthew notes. This episode becomes the setting of the following two sections, and lets the reader see them as reactions to **the kingdom of God.** On **authority,** see notes at 4:32; on **power,** see notes at 1:17. **(V)**

[3] The twelve were to go depending completely upon God. Their business was urgent, and the time short, so they were not to delay for special preparation (see 10:4). Mark says they were commanded to **take nothing** except a **staff** (contrasted to Luke's **no staff**). One ingenious reconciliation suggests the words for "except" (Mark) and **no** (Luke) represent similar Aramaic words, and that in transmission Jesus' exact words somehow became confused into these two variants. An easier solution is that Mark's account meant to take only the **staff** they had, whereas Luke's account referred to taking another **staff.** The basic meaning in all three gospels is "go as you are."

The **bag** may have been a beggar's pouch. They were not to beg, as pagan missionaries of the day sometimes did. The tunic ("coat" in 3:11 and 6:29) was a short-sleeved, knee-length garment, held at the waist by a girdle. The idea was not to take a change of clothes. Josephus (*Wars* II, viii, 125ff.) records similar practices among the Essenes of the day. There would come a later time when the disciples of

Shake Off Dust   LUKE 9:3-8

⁴And whatever house you enter, stay there, and from there depart. ⁵And wherever they do not receive you, when you leave that town shake off the dust from your feet as a testimony against them." ⁶And they departed and went through the villages, preaching the gospel and healing everywhere.

⁷Now Herod the tetrarch heard of all that was done, and he was perplexed, because it was said by some that John had been raised from the dead, ⁸by some that Elijah had appeared, and by others that one of the old prophets had risen.

Jesus, soon to face troubles, would require a **bag** and a **sword** (22:36). (VIII)

[4-6] These instructions are recorded in more detail by Matthew. The disciples were to rely on hospitality along the way (cf. 10:5-7). This was not difficult in Palestine, where the strong Eastern idea of the necessity of hospitality prevailed; yet Jesus warned they might be rejected. They were to **shake off the dust** of those towns rejecting them as a sign (see notes at 5:14). Jews would do this upon re-entering Palestine after being in a Gentile area. The people refusing the message were to be treated as having no part in the people of God. Their ministry was **preaching and healing,** in extension of Jesus' work.

Herod Thinks Jesus is John, Risen, 9:7-9 (Matt. 14:1f.; Mark 6:14-16)

[7, 8] This episode has been entitled "the power of a guilty conscience." Perhaps **Herod** had heard of Jesus because of the efforts of the twelve. Now the news was startling enough to cause him to be **perplexed** (a word only Luke uses in the New Testament: Acts 2:12; 5:24; 10:17). According to Matthew Herod thought **John,** whom he had put to death, was risen. Luke, who does not record the death of John but only his imprisonment (3:18-20), attributes the report to **others.** Though **John** worked no miracles during his life, it might be expected that if he came back from the grave

LUKE 9:7-12 *Herod and John*

⁹ Herod said, "John I beheaded; but who is this about whom I hear such things?" And he sought to see him.

¹⁰ On their return the apostles told him what they had done. And he took them and withdrew apart to a city called Bethsaida. ¹¹ When the crowds learned it, they followed him; and he welcomed them and spoke to them of the kingdom of God, and cured those who had need of healing. ¹² Now the day began to wear away; and the twelve came and said to him, "Send the crowd away, to go into the villages and country round about, to lodge and get provisions; for we are here in a lonely place." ¹³ But he said to them, "You give them something to eat." They said, "We have no more than

---

he would have the sort of supernatural power which Jesus was exhibiting. There was also a similarity of message which might encourage the **John**-Jesus identity. Another opinion was that Jesus was **Elijah** (see Mal. 4:5f.). **Elijah** did not die, but was taken to heaven in a fiery chariot. Some suggested Jesus was **one of the old** (the earlier) **prophets.**

[9] Because of his responsibility for John's death, **Herod** was especially anxious about Jesus, to see if he were **John** or not. His desire prepares the reader for the episode in 23:8-12. How did Luke know all these details about **Herod**? Apparently they became part of the tradition of the church, perhaps learned from such people as Chuza (8:3). (IV, VI)

Feeding the Five Thousand, 9:10-17 (Matt. 14:13-21; Mark 6:31-44; John 6:1-13)

[10, 11] This is the only miracle common to all four gospels, and forms the climax of the Galilean ministry. Subsequently, though his death was a year away (according to John's indication the feeding was at Passover), Jesus spoke more of his coming passion. The twelve returned, but none of the gospels record Jesus' reaction to their work (cf. 10:17). **Bethsaida** was a small town at the north end of the sea of Galilee, across the Jordan, east of Herod's jurisdiction. On **kingdom,** see notes at 1:33.

[12-15] Mark mentions that the **food** would cost two

Meal Blessing   LUKE 9:15-19

five loaves and two fish—unless we are to go and buy food for all these people." [14] For there were about five thousand men. And he said to his disciples, "Make them sit down in companies, about fifty each." [15] And they did so, and made them all sit down. [16] And taking the five loaves and the two fish he looked up to heaven, and blessed and broke them, and gave them to the disciples to set before the crowd. [17] And all ate and were satisfied. And they took up what was left over, twelve baskets of broken pieces.

[18] Now it happened that as he was praying alone the disciples were with him; and he asked them, "Who do the people say that I am?" [19] And they answered, "John the Baptist;

---

hundred denarii. No merchant would have provisions for so many even if one could be found, and the price would be prohibitive—over half a year's wages (see Matt. 20:2). Jesus may have brought this entire matter up to remind them of what God's power could do, as the catch of fish (5:1-10) made the same point to Peter and his companions. (Cf. 2 Kings 4:42-44.) (VI)

[16, 17] Jesus may have employed the standard meal blessing (usually uttered by the host at the meal), but here the text seems to imply it unleashed special power. The word for **basket** (*kophinos*) indicates a wallet commonly carried by Jews to keep from having to buy bread from Gentiles. In the story of the feeding of the four thousand the word is *spuris*, a much larger basket, big enough to hold a man (Matt. 15:37; Mark 8:8).

This wonder could remind the people of the manna in the wilderness, and John makes the connection specific. The early church may well have connected this in some way with the Lord's Supper (see John 6). Luke stresses the meal motif frequently in his gospel (notes 5:27).

The Confession and First Passion Prediction, 9:18-22 (Matt. 16:13-23; Mark 8:27-33)

[18, 19] The Galilean ministry reached a climax, as Luke

LUKE 9:19-20 — *Jesus' Identity*

but others say, Elijah; and others, that one of the old prophets has risen." [20] And he said to them, "But who do you say that I am?" And Peter answered, "The Christ of God."

---

records it, with the feeding. It is followed by the great confession, which was the significant turning point of Jesus' career, as he thereafter consciously pointed his way to Jerusalem. Luke bypasses a number of events recorded in Mark 6:45-8:26, apparently because they did not suit his purpose. Thus he does not give a geographical or other background for the great confession. John and Luke agree in placing the confession immediately after the feeding (John 6:66-69).

Only Luke records that Jesus was **praying** at this time, as if to say one reason they recognized who he was was from his prayer life (see notes at 1:10 and cf. 24:30f.). When he asked regarding popular opinions of himself, Jesus received the same answers indicated in the Herod incident (9:8). No popular speculation had seen him as the Messiah. Jesus knew the answers to his questions but was leading **the disciples** to verbalize their recognition. (VI)

[20] Jesus now asked, "But you" (the Greek gives this emphasis), "what **do you say?**" It was important that his disciples should understand him. His question implied that there was more to be said than had been already revealed or was reflected in the public opinions. Had they read the signs aright, especially in view of what they must go through for him? How much would they stake on their concept of Jesus?

Peter sprung to the answer, perhaps responding out of a flash of insight. Did this request pull previous impressions together in his mind and produce at the moment a climactic recognition? Or, perhaps the group had been coming to this conclusion, and **Peter** spoke their corporate feelings. In any event, the impact of the confession must have been great.

The confession in Mark states the bare fact that he was **the Christ**. Luke is more detailed, and Matthew's "Son of

Suffering Messiah   **LUKE 9:20-22**

[21] But he charged and commanded them to tell this to no one, [22] saying, "The Son of man must suffer many things, and be rejected by the elders and chief priests and scribes, and be killed, and on the third day be raised."

---

the Living God" is the most complete. Here is Luke's first presentation of the adult Jesus as **the Christ** (see notes at 2:11) in which Jesus himself encouraged and approved the recognition. Note the previous confessions about Jesus in Luke 3:16f., 22; 4:3, 9, 18-21, 22, 32, 36, 41; 5:5, 8, 15, 21, 24; 6:5; 7:16, 20-23, 34, 49; 8:28; 9:1f., 7. The kingdom does not involve reciting a creed but knowing a person. Thus were fulfilled the words of 8:10. (V)

[21, 22] Here again Jesus forbade men to tell about him. One reason may have been because a messiahship involving suffering would not be accepted and understood by the Jews. At this point Matthew is more detailed. After Jesus' passion his true nature would be more fully revealed and understood.

Here again Jesus called himself **the Son of man** (see notes at 5:24), tying the idea to suffering. This is the first clear passion saying in Luke (though compare 5:35). Other passion references are found at 9:31, 44f., (51), 12:50; 13:32f.; (16:30); 17:25; 18:31-34; (20:13-15); 22:15, 19, 21f., 37, 42; (24:6f.). These words would force the disciples to revamp their messianic concept. Yet even with this they still did not understand (9:44f.). Jesus indicated his suffering was a divine necessity (**must suffer**). He would **be rejected,** a word cognate to one used of the scrutiny an elected magistrate had to undergo at Athens to see if he was qualified for office. Jesus was scrutinized—and **rejected**. He knew what would happen and had the added psychological burden of having to anticipate it. But in accepting rejection, Jesus made discipleship a thing man must choose freely, knowing the cost of it. God's purposes were such that what would look like defeat would eventuate in victory, for Jesus would **be raised on the third day**. The religious leaders who would try to

LUKE 9:21-24 — Cross Bearing

> [23] And he said to all, "If any man would come after me, let him deny himself and take up his cross daily and follow me. [24] For whoever would save his life will lose it; and whoever loses his life for my sake, he will save it.

eliminate Jesus were those who ought to have been the first to accept him. (II, III, IV, V, VI, VII)

The Conditions of Discipleship, 9:23-27 (Matt. 16:24-28; Mark 8:34-9:1)

[23] Though spoken **to all,** these words would have special significance to the apostles, because of the revelation at the great confession. Those who would follow a suffering Messiah must be prepared to face similar experiences.

Self-denial (the same word is used later of Peter's denial of the Lord) has as its prototype Jesus himself (see Phil. 2:5-11). This is the first mention of the **cross** in Luke. The Jews had known of hundreds of rebels who had been crucified in Palestine (Josephus, *Antiquities* XVII, x, 295). Cicero said the very name of the **cross** should not be told of, seen, or heard in good Roman society. It was a cruel torture instrument, reserved for the worst sort of criminals. Thus Jesus implied the manner of his death, though the disciples would not have grasped his meaning till later. The **cross** was to be borne **daily** (only in Luke). Jesus doubtless meant things borne for him that would be as difficult as literally bearing a **cross,** or things that could lead to such an ignominious death. **Daily** implies the persistence of discipleship. These were not just the **daily** troubles of life, as popular thought sometimes supposes, but rather the willingness to accept hardship for Christ's sake. Cf. Matthew 10:38; Luke 14:27.

[24] The ideas expressed in the comments on the previous verse are here expressed by Jesus in yet another form (note parallels in Matt. 10:39; Luke 17:33; and John 12:25). The language is paradoxical. One seems to go against a goal

Coming in Glory LUKE 9:24-27

²⁵ For what does it profit a man if he gains the whole world and loses or forfeits himself? ²⁶ For whoever is ashamed of me and my words, of him will the Son of man be ashamed when he comes in his glory and the glory of the Father and of the holy angels. ²⁷ But I tell you truly, there are some standing here who will not taste death before they see the kingdom of God."

---

to accomplish it. But Jesus' words are true because he argues from a transcendent order. One oriented to the spiritual realm would know their truth, since they can only be understood by faith. Such a person would be engrafted into the resurrection self of Christ, thus saving **his life.** (I, II, VI)

[25] One's essential being, his higher spiritual side, is more important than all possessions. These words could have had reference to any physical kingdom expectations, but certainly their meaning was much broader than that. They offer encouragement to those who would learn that following Jesus would be difficult. The quest would be eminently worth the price paid.

[26] Jesus' coming (here mentioned for the first time in Luke) would be with **glory of Father, Son, and angels** (on **glory,** see notes at 2:9). The disciples were to know when it became difficult to confess Jesus and his **words** that their actions would have eternal consequences. Whatever might happen to them, there would be a victorious culmination for those who persevered. On **Son of man,** see notes at 5:24. (IV, VI, VII)

[27] Mark adds that **the kingdom** would come "with power." Luke mentions **the kingdom** coming with power in Acts 1:5-8. No signs are given at this point for ways in which **the kingdom** (see notes at 1:33) might be recognized, but they would be given subsequently (24:49; Acts 1:5-8). Acts 1:5-8 and 2:1-4 point to Pentecost as fulfilling Jesus' words. This would fit the requirement that some then living would **see the kingdom.** (IV) The transfiguration which follows was an anticipation of the kingdom glory of Jesus.

LUKE 9:28-31   *Transfiguration*

[28] Now about eight days after these sayings he took with him Peter and John and James, and went up on the mountain to pray. [29] And as he was praying, the appearance of his countenance was altered, and his raiment became dazzling white. [30] And behold, two men talked with him, Moses and Elijah, [31] who appeared in glory and spoke of his departure, which he was to accomplish at Jerusalem.

The Transfiguration, 9:28-36 (Matt. 17:1-8; Mark 9:2-8)

[28, 29] Matthew and Mark have the transfiguration six **days** after the confession, rather than **eight.** They probably count only the intervening **days,** whereas Luke counts also the **days** of the two terminal events. Luke's **about** rules out the need for any scientific precision. The mountain is not known, though both Hermon and Tabor have been suggested. The disciples had confessed Jesus' true nature, and now three of them (cf. 8:51) were to see it. Only Luke says Jesus **went up to pray** (see notes at 1:10). **He** prayed and was changed into a glorified being—one might say his heavenly glory was made visible (cf. Ex. 34:29-35; Acts 9:3). Since Luke does not use the word "transfigured" to name this experience, he describes it more fully. He probably avoided the term *metamorphoō* because Gentile readers might mistakenly connect it with the metamorphoses of heathen deities. (IV)

[30, 31] This mysterious event involved the other world communicating with this one to bring a message. The law **(Moses)** and the prophets **(Elijah)** now turn to the accomplishment of Jesus' work. Unless the apostles were given the power to recognize **Moses** and **Elijah** with the vision, the whole event would have been meaningless. Note that in verses 8 and 19 Jesus was thought to be **Elijah,** but **Elijah** here witnesses to Jesus.

Verse 31 is unique to Luke, and it makes the passage a passion and victory saying (cf. 9:22). The **departure** would

Exodus   LUKE 9:31-33

³²Now Peter and those who were with him were heavy with sleep but kept awake, and they saw his glory and the two men who stood with him. ³³And as the men were parting from him, Peter said to Jesus, "Master, it is well that we are here; let us make three booths, one for you and one for Moses and one for Elijah"—not knowing what he said.

---

be an "exodus" (the Greek term). This would suggest the entire cluster of ideas around that event in the Old Testament, including seeing Jesus as a new **Moses** leading the people from their captivity to sin. The exodus would also include Jesus' resurrection, for it was there he secured freedom from death and sin. The trip to **Jerusalem**, then, was no casual thing but was as significant as the Israelite march out of Egypt. Jesus' reference to **Jerusalem** was the first connection of the city with the passion, and seems to point to 9:51 (see notes 2:22). Again the disciples were apprised of the connection between suffering and **glory**. (IV, VI, VII)

[32] This verse, unique to Luke, seems to indicate the experience took place at night. Either the disciples remained **awake** or were thoroughly wakened from their sleepiness by the events (cf. Matt. 26:43). **Glory** is characteristically used in the New Testament to refer to the reality of the new age (see notes at 2:9; cf. John 1:14; Rom. 8:18ff.; 2 Cor. 4:17; Heb. 2:9f.; 1 Peter 1:21; 4:14; 5:4).

[33] Peter's address **to Jesus** is a case of all three gospels giving a speech in which different words were used to address the Lord. Luke uses *epistata* (see notes at 5:5), Mark "rabbi," and Matthew *kurie* (Lord). Perhaps **Peter** wished to build **booths** to establish the permanence of the scene and preserve the glory and rapture, as the glory was associated with the Tabernacle in the Exodus story. Another suggestion is that it was the time for the Feast of **Booths**, and **Peter** wished to keep the feast on the mountain with **Moses** and **Elijah**—a thought to thrill the heart of any Israelite (despite the fact the feast was a Jerusalem celebration). But

LUKE 9:33-36   *Hear Jesus*

³⁴As he said this, a cloud came and overshadowed them; and they were afraid as they entered the cloud. ³⁵And a voice came out of the cloud, saying, "This is my Son, my Chosen;*ᵈ* listen to him!" ³⁶And when the voice had spoken, Jesus was found alone. And they kept silence and told no one in those days anything of what they had seen.

  ᵈ Other ancient authorities read *my Beloved*

---

he did not know **what he said**—perhaps indicating that he was not aware that he was beholding a heavenly mystery which could not be bound in earthly forms. (VI)

[34, 35] This **cloud** came, as if to say, "not in a booth, but in glory, is their dwelling place." The total experience well illustrates the awesomeness of the holy when it intrudes upon human experience (cf. Peter's reaction in 5:8; and see notes at 1:12).

For **my Chosen** Matthew, Mark, and some texts of Luke have "my Beloved." The meaning is not drastically altered in either event (contrast 23:35). Lying behind these words were the messianic pictures in Psalm 2:7 and Isaiah 42:1, as at the baptismal announcement (see notes at 3:22; and cf. John 12:28-30; 2 Peter 1:17f.).

The decree to **listen** may have its background in the "prophet" of Deuteronomy 18:15-19, since Christ is identified with that figure several places in the New Testament (John 6:14; Acts 3:22; 7:37). The point was, "Now hear Jesus as the supreme authoritative voice." The decree did not necessarily abrogate the law and prophets, but it did indicate the note that was to be paid to Jesus' teachings. Primary attention should be given him even over the great documents of the Jewish faith. The heavenly announcement may also be an expression of divine pleasure that the **Son** had chosen the way of suffering. (IV)

[36] The lesson made, **Jesus** was once again seen in the form of his humiliation. In Matthew and Mark the next section says **Jesus** told them to be silent until his resurrection. Luke simply has **they told no one in those days**. (V)

Disciples' Failure LUKE 9:37-40

³⁷ On the next day, when they had come down from the mountain, a great crowd met him. ³⁸ And behold, a man from the crowd cried, "Teacher, I beg you to look upon my son, for he is my only child; ³⁹ and behold, a spirit seizes him, and he suddenly cries out; it convulses him till he foams, and shatters him, and will hardly leave him. ⁴⁰ And I begged your disciples to cast it out, but they could not."

A Spirit-Possessed Boy Healed, 9:37-43a (Matt. 17:14-21; Mark 9:14-29)

[37-39] This exorcism took place **next day,** because the transfiguration was at night (cf. 6:12, 17; 19:37; 22:39 for other **mountain** experiences of Jesus). From the hilltop they returned to a world of suffering and need. Had Peter's request to stay behind been heeded, this healing could not have taken place. Yet the Lord had to be in the drama of human existence. So after two episodes in isolation, Jesus was with the crowds again.

Luke alone records it was an **only child** (see 7:12; 8:42), and this detail adds pathos to the story. Luke's account says the **child** cried out, while Mark speaks of a dumb spirit. Probably the **child** made inarticulate sounds. Matthew describes him as an epileptic. The seizures persisted to trouble the youth **(they hardly leave him).** In this story, as in the rest of the chapter, one sees Luke's skillful depiction of the contrast between confirmation and rejection of Jesus' claims. On **beg,** see notes at 5:12. (VI)

[40] The man may have sought Jesus' help and, failing to find him, turned to those nearest him. It is not necessary to think he appealed to the nine apostles left below. However, if these were the ones unable to exorcise, one might suppose their lack of faith made it impossible for them to exercise the power Jesus had given them earlier (9:1). While Christ was seen in his supernal form, his disciples were frustrated by the powers of darkness. On **begged,** see notes at 5:12.

LUKE 9:41-43 — *Demon Cast Out*

⁴¹ Jesus answered, "O faithless and perverse generation, how long am I to be with you and bear with you? Bring your son here." ⁴² While he was coming, the demon tore him and convulsed him. But Jesus rebuked the unclean spirit, and healed the boy, and gave him back to his father. ⁴³ And all were astonished at the majesty of God.

But while they were all marvelling at everything he did, he said to his disciples,

---

[41] **Jesus** may have rebuked all those present (especially the crowd that might have gathered just out of curiosity). On his language compare Numbers 14:27; Deuteronomy 32:5; and Matthew 16:4. Or the rebuke may have been mainly for the disciples (since often those who came for healing had to have faith to come at all), with the implication that if they believed they could have made the lad well. Mark 9:29 indicates the failure to heal was due to improper attitude—they preferred argument to prayer. **Jesus** may well have been disturbed because a preoccupation with signs and wonders kept them from seeing the significance of his mission and the kingdom message. His words **how long . . .** seem an impatient sigh for that time when his earthly task would be over and his victory complete. (VI)

[42, 43a] A great deal of material which Luke omits is found at this point in Mark. Mark's main point in telling the story concerns faith, whereas Luke is more interested in this messianic sign prior to another passion saying (seeing the hand of **God** in the act, cf. Acts 2:22). Luke also omits the subsequent words of Jesus regarding faith. He is the only writer, however, to trace the crowd's reaction, indicating his account is more centered in the impact of the person of Jesus. As the **demon** departed, in one last malevolent act he **tore the boy**. **Tore** is a word sometimes used of boxers and wrestlers punishing their opponents. The **demon** left, but **the boy** still needed healing (cf. 4:35).

Passion Predicted   LUKE 9:43-46

⁴⁴"Let these words sink into your ears; for the Son of man is to be delivered into the hands of men." ⁴⁵But they did not understand this saying, and it was concealed from them, that they should not perceive it; and they were afraid to ask him about this saying.

⁴⁶And an argument arose among them as to which of them was the greatest.

A Further Passion Prediction, 9:43b-45 (Matt. 17:22f.; Mark 9:30-32)

[43b, 44] Jesus' **let these words sink . . .** gave even greater emphasis to their lack of insight, as if they heard his words without understanding them. So he gave this further prediction of the passion to the larger group of disciples (see notes at 9:22). (VII)

[45] Several explanations might be offered for the concealment, which is simply another way of describing their lack of understanding (see 18:34; 24:45; and 2:50; John 16:18f.). It may be that **they** could not conceive of a Messiah in such a way and thought Jesus was wrong. In Jewish thought the Messiah was not a figure who would die. Perhaps they were afraid of his mysterious words and conduct. **They** might not have wanted to hear more, since the announcement was one they did not want to believe. Whatever the explanation, the oscillation between acceptance and rejection continued, even with the disciples. (V, VI)

The Dispute About Greatness, 9:46-48 (Matt. 18:1-5; Mark 9:33-37; cf. also Luke 22:24-27)

[46] The **argument** may have been called **forth** by the special privilege given Peter, James and John at the transfiguration. The whole situation illustrates the obtuseness of which Jesus spoke in the preceding paragraph. Had the disciples gained the inner meaning of the passion sayings, such a dispute would not have occurred. They still seemed to think of a physical kingdom (cf. Matt. 18:1).

LUKE 9:47-50 *Lesson of a Child*

⁴⁷But when Jesus perceived the thought of their hearts, he took a child and put him by his side, ⁴⁸and said to them, "Whoever receives this child in my name receives me, and whoever receives me receives him who sent me; for he who is least among you all is the one who is great."

⁴⁹John answered, "Master, we saw a man casting out demons in your name, and we forbade him, because he does not follow with us." ⁵⁰But Jesus said to him, "Do not forbid him; for he that is not against you is for you."

[47, 48] Receiving **a child** could mean that the honored disciple is the one who humbles himself to be concerned even with children, or that they should be childlike, so when they were received for Christ's sake that would be enough. See Matthew 10:40, as well as other "children" sayings in Mark 10:15; Luke 10:21; and 17:2. Even **a child** would be adequate to bear witness if he went **in** Christ's **name** on God's commission. **In my name** means with regard for **Jesus** and who he is. They were to think about the **name** in which they went, not about themselves. To stress the point, **Jesus** made his usages of the word **me** emphatic. The true secret of greatness was the direct opposite of what they sought. **Jesus** could not have confuted them more frontally. (III)

The Strange Exorcist, 9:49, 50 (Mark 9:38-41)

[49] This might have been a secret disciple to whom Jesus had imparted power (cf. 10:17) and whom the others did not know. Matthew 7:21 notes people who claimed to exorcise **in** Jesus' **name** whom he did not know. But they had not done his will, and here the next verse implies the contrary.

[50] Mark's account indicates the man actually exorcised. Contrast with this passage Matthew 12:30 and Luke 11:23. Each of these sayings has to be given meaning in its specific context. The man in the present case was not

An Unknown Ally — LUKE 9:50

neutral, as in the other passages, though his discipleship might have been as yet incomplete. In Matthew 12 and Luke 11 Jesus gave a test by which a disciple was to try himself, while here he gave one by which to try others.

The idea is that unless there is open hostility, the person should be regarded as an ally. With issues coming to a head shortly, and opposition intensifying, the disciples would need every friend, for it would not be easy to favor Christ. Thus Luke sharpens the acceptance-rejection motif of this chapter.

With this the Galilean ministry ends. At this point the mission of Jesus and the nature of the kingdom were still somewhat of an enigma. Jesus' words clarifying the situation had been mostly misunderstood.